CLERGY IN THE CROSS FIRE

CLERGY IN THE CROSS FIRE

Coping with Role Conflicts in the Ministry

by
DONALD P. SMITH

THE WESTMINSTER PRESS
Philadelphia

Book design by Dorothy Alden Smith

Published by The Westminster Press ®

Philadelphia, Pennsylvania

PRINTED IN THE UNITED STATES OF AMERICA

Library of Congress Cataloging in Publication Data

Smith, Donald P., 1922–
    Clergy in the cross fire.

    Bibliography: p.
    1. Clergy—Office. I. Title.
BV660.2.S623   253'.2   72–8009
ISBN 0–664–20964–5 (Cloth)
ISBN 0–664–24963–9 (Paper)

Contents

Expect it free prof./vol. institution.
Increase Communication?
Deal directly with conflict.
Negotiate new understandings
Utilize the system.
Support grps.
Area ministry
Career clustg.
Maximize the marriage

PART II

WHAT TO DO
  ABOUT ROLE AMBIGUITY AND CONFLICT   81

Caught in the Cross Fire!

From the first moment a young pastor steps into the pulpit or presides at a board meeting he is caught in the cross fire of conflicting expectations for the ministry.

We are all aware that there is widespread confusion as to what the church is all about. Who is a minister anyway, and what should he really be doing? Is he the benevolent, white-haired gentleman with backward collar that elderly Miss Jones knew as a little girl in a Midwestern parish, or is he the long-haired, flaming reformer whom the young radical would like to find in her corner when the battle gets under way?

Conflicting Expectations

If ministers preach on social issues, someone is sure to tell them to "stick to religion." If they don't, someone else will slip away from the church because they aren't relevant. On the one hand they may be confused over why they are in the ministry and where their priorities lie. On the other hand, they may have developed a very clear picture indeed of the way they are going to spend their lives and of what they are going to do for the world. If they move confidently in one direction, someone is almost certain to rise up and challenge their right to do so. If they fail to move, some will get restless because they are drifting. They are supposed to be paragons and experts in everything. To fall short in any aspect of their ministry is to become a target for criticism, even though their performance in other areas may be outstanding. (74.) And so the impossible demands of universal expertise may lead to feelings of inadequacy, self-derogation, and guilt.

Church officers may be divided on whether or not certain forms of worship are unalterable; not to mention their division on more vital issues, such as poverty, racism, and war. If a minister has an international perspective or does not "ring the changes" on the patriotic line, his loyalty may be suspect. If he comes into the service of the Lord with a sense of divine calling, it will probably not be very long until someone makes it clear that after all, his task is to serve the congregation and do what they want. Is the minister not their employee?

To whom shall he listen? The pastor carries on his professional career in the midst of mixed signals and conflicting expectations. The national leaders talk in terms of the local church existing for the sake of the world, and therefore . . . being essentially world-oriented and deeply concerned about the problems of society. . . . The judicatories closer to the local church give off mixed signals. They are more conscious of the need of institutional success, and keep the pastor's eyes focused on more money and more members but at the same time constantly feed him signals and models which suggest that institutional success is not what it is all about after all. This double kind of incongruent signal therefore contributes to the pastor's role confusion. The lay people . . . just want a peaceful church to go to, conflict free—a place for comfort during the grinding routine and a place of refuge when crisis comes. And most of the laity bring the criterion for judging success (organizational maintenance) into the judgment of whether the clergyman is or is not doing a good job.

Which master shall he serve? Within his congregation are people of many different political persuasions; children, young people, middle-aged people; the politically active, the politically quiescent; the far-outs and the far-ins. Also present are the real estate agents and the poor; the business community with stakes in what is, and the social action group which wants to change everything. They all want something different of him, and in times of controversy they often feel themselves betrayed by their pastor. (74:120–121.)

It Matters to Many

Nor is the cross fire of conflicting expectations limited to the pastorates of the young. The mature minister of many years' experience may suddenly find the "young Turks" in control of his judicatory. They make insistent demands that he take strong action in his congregation along rather clear-cut and specified lines as proof of his loyalty to the gospel of Jesus Christ. To fail to do so is to find a waning influence in the courts of the denomination. People in his congregation somehow do not respond as they once did, and he wonders why. Change seems to undermine those things which he has treasured most, and to threaten his ministry, and thus his own being.

For most clergymen today, role ambiguity and role conflict are not matters of mere academic curiosity. Rather, these are the heart of the most difficult problems that the minister faces. Many voices speak with insistence in his ear.

What is a minister? He is an evangelist. He is a preacher. He is a priest. He is a religious administrator. He is a social reformer. He is a director of worthwhile enterprises for the community. He is a species of amateur psychiatrist. He is an educator. He is an interpreter of life, somewhat in the fashion of a poet. He is the custodian of the values of democratic civilization. He is a man of superior wisdom and virtue whose task each week is to show men and women how to live more wisely and virtuously. Is it any wonder that young ministers, and some not so young, find themselves dragged in a dozen different directions as they try to fulfill the claims of the ministry? (126:17–18.)

He is so many things to so many people, he often gets lost in the maze of his own roles, and no wonder. . . .

In other words, he is an octopus. This phrase exactly describes the minister's life. He is into everything. This is both the glory and the pain of his calling. He cannot possibly do justice to everything he is called upon to do, so some of his "tentacles" will reach farther than others, and some will hold more tenaciously to one thing than another, and some will atrophy because of no use at all. He will need a sharp mind for following his far-flung and varied interests, lest one or more of them be neglected, or left dangling with no relationship to what is going on in his life. (81:90, 103–104.)

What Can I Do About It?

Many ministers discover ways to reduce ambiguity and conflict in the expectations of others, or are fortunate enough to find themselves in a church where the conflict can be channeled creatively toward more effective ministry. Others bear the pain as long as they can, and if they are able, move to another congregation (more congenial to their ministry, they hope), or even leave the pastorate altogether. "How long should I continue the battle?" one of them asks. "When does it cease to be 'the good fight of faith' and become instead destructive obstinacy? How can I deal with conflicting expectations so I am not blown about with every wind that blows?" What is role conflict? Why is ambiguity so enervating? And what can be done about these things by the pastor, by his presbytery, conference, or diocese, and by his denomination? These are some of the questions to which this book addresses itself from the perspective of social psychology and in the light of recent research.

The Contribution of Research

Samuel Blizzard's classic studies of clergy role conflict and ambiguity in the mid-1950's have in many respects been confirmed by more recent research which they stimulated. Meanwhile, new patterns of ministry have emerged with accompanying new expectations. These must be taken into account while recognizing that older expectations of the clergyman's task do not change quickly. They persist for the vast majority of parishioners. As a consequence, church people in the 1970's bring to their relationship with their minister a much wider range of images than they did in the 1950's.

Take, for example, the image of the minister as a social and political activist. In the last few years this has emerged with vigor as an important new dimension of ministry to be welcomed enthusiastically by some parishioners and to be vigorously condemned by others. To put it mildly, this new role possibility has for many ministers considerably increased the likelihood of role conflict. This book attempts to reflect the broad range of role expectations (both traditional and modern) that now complicates and modifies the role picture represented by earlier research.

Recent research has explored much-needed solutions to role conflicts and ambiguities. Meanwhile, a great deal of advice to the clergy has been written by countless authors; frequently it reflects the personal experience and convictions of a particular pastor or professor.

However, there appears to be no systematic compilation of research for use by the minister himself and the church officers who work closely with him. (97 and 98.) There is no summary of suggestions growing out of that research. Nor have the insights of role theory and of related study of other professions been applied to the ministry in a comprehensive and convenient form. Church officers are almost entirely without help in understanding the demands that are made upon their minister. They should be provided with clues on how they can work with him more effectively. This needs to be done with due consideration for the corrective steps that the church itself as a total system must take if there is to be any significant reduction in role conflict and ambiguity. In view of the particular role problems that the clergyman faces, such material might prove very helpful to the church and its leadership if it were available.

This book makes no pretense of being a complete or comprehensive interpretation of the ministry. It does seek to make some sense of the considerable body of theory and research that is now available. It seeks to integrate and summarize the valuable work of many persons. It tries to take relevant concepts of ministry, interpret them to pastor and people, and apply them to the practical concerns of the church.

First, the principal findings of research on the minister's roles will be summarized and analyzed in such a way as to clarify the nature of his dilemmas. Second, some relevant highlights of role theory and some results of studies on the management and reduction of role conflict will be examined and applied. Third, support mechanisms, procedures, and structures that exist or might be created to help clergy deal with role conflicts will be suggested. Finally, the possibilities of goal-setting and performance review will be elaborated as two specially promising areas for clergy initiative in the reduction of role confusion and conflict.

What About Women Clergy?

Before the close of these introductory comments, an apology to women clergy may be in order. The author is keenly aware of an important dilemma in dealing with the concerns of women in the church. Most of the presuppositions that are made about the clergy grow out of a male-dominated ministry. Women have had—and continue to have—great difficulty, first in winning the right to be ordained, and then in securing calls to the pastorate. It appears that even women in the pews, who certainly constitute a majority of the church membership (as they do of the population), have not yet been aroused to the place where they will assert the importance of equal opportunity for women in the ministry. These concerns are not adequately reflected in this book.

In these pages there is frequent use of the masculine third-person pronoun in the generic sense. Within the current limitations of the English language, it would be very awkward to do otherwise. It is hoped that this will be interpreted not as reinforcing male chauvinism in the church, but as illustrative of limitations which have yet to be overcome. Although effort has been made to avoid exclusively male-oriented illustrations of role dilemmas or role solutions, undoubtedly a woman minister could find ways in which this might have been dealt with more sensitively. The fact that so overwhelming a majority of ministers are men makes even this very difficult.

Bibliographical Notes

Notes in the text referring to bibliographical sources are indicated by numbers within parentheses. When there is only one number, it refers to a book or other source in the bibliography, listed under that number. A number that follows a colon indicates the page number or numbers of the work cited. Thus (76) would refer to *Organizational Stress: Studies in Role Conflict and Ambiguity,* by Robert L. Kahn, which is item 76 in the bibliography, and (56:34-35) would refer to pages 34 to 35 in *Profession: Minister,* by James D. Glasse.

Acknowledgments

A writer is inclined to express more voluminous appreciation than his reader will have patience to read. Deep gratitude is expressed to a host of people who have shared their wisdom and experience in conversation or in writing. These are listed in the back of the book as "Consultants." In addition, special thanks goes to the Commission on Ecumenical Mission and Relations, which provided the sabbatical time that made possible the necessary study and writing. Donald Super and Kenneth Herrold of Teachers College, Columbia University, were particularly helpful in stimulating my thinking and guiding my study. Edgar Mills has made many helpful suggestions, and his ideas have had a clear influence on numerous works on which this book has drawn.

Lorraine Mead has spent many hours of meticulous labor in typing and retyping the manuscripts, in organizing the bibliography, and in writing the scores of letters required for this study. Without her dedicated and professional service this book would never have seen the light of day.

Finally, this book is dedicated to my wife, Verna, whose loving partnership in marriage and in ministry has inspired and enabled such creativity as I have been able to bring to this and other projects.

D. P. S.

Glen Rock, New Jersey

PART
I
UNDERSTANDING
ROLE CONFLICT AND AMBIGUITY

When one is confronted by the expectations of those related to him or is under the tension of conflicting expectations, it helps to step back and take a look at what is happening. Understanding is the prelude to intelligent action. Part I will analyze role ambiguity, conflict, flexibility, and overload as the basis for a consideration of the alternative courses of action to be discussed in Part II.

CHAPTER 1

What Are We Talking About?

Since some of the discussion that follows in subsequent chapters makes use of several technical terms from role theory, this chapter will define those terms and illustrate the definitions from the experience of the clergy.

What Is a Role?

A *role* consists of one or more recurrent or patterned activities of the *player*, activities that involve corresponding expectations on the part of others who are related to the player. The term is borrowed from the theater and is used to make clear that the expected behavior relates to the *position* of the focal person and not to the *person* who occupies that position. (123 and 77.) For example, the minister is expected by his congregation to conduct a worship service and to preach a sermon on Sunday morning. Whatever person is called to be the minister will be expected to preach. That is one of his roles. A priest, on the other hand, may be expected to conduct mass, whether or not he preaches a sermon.

"Ministers Ought to . . ."

Expectations are an essential part of the role concept. Each role has expectations related to it, such as what a person should do or refrain from doing, how one should behave in relation to others, what kind of person one should be, and even what one should think and believe. (76.) Congregations may expect that a sermon not be longer than 20 minutes, or that the service should in no case close after 12 noon. They also have rather particular ideas about what they like in the way a minister preaches. In fact, they give so much weight to this that pulpit nominating committees go to considerable trouble to listen to a preacher before they will agree on recommending him. There are numerous specific expectations related to the role of preacher.

Senders and Receivers

The one who expects something of the role player is sometimes called a *role sender*. The role player or focal person is also called the *role receiver*. These terms emphasize the fact that role expectations involve communication, both verbal and nonverbal. A role always involves reciprocal expectations of both sender and receiver. (138.) Just as the parishioner expects things of the minister, such as preaching, so the minister expects things of the parishioner, such as participation in worship. These mutual expectations may be commonly understood, as in the case of preaching, or they may need to be communicated subtly, or even explicitly. The clarity with which a role sender communicates his expectations, or with which the receiver understands them, can cause either role clarity on the one hand, or role confusion or ambiguity on the other. (77.) This will be looked at more carefully later.

Role Pressures

The process of communication involved in role-sending and role-receiving is more than the transmission of information regarding the role sender's desires. In fact, role expectations are perhaps more accurately described as "role pressures," since the sender is really trying to influence the receiver to conform to his expectations. Naturally the attempts to influence will vary in intensity from one person or group to another, depending upon the importance of the issues to the sender, the resistance encountered, etc. The sender may not even realize that he is seeking to influence the focal person. Usually role expectations carry some role pressure with them, although the relationship is not necessarily a direct one. (76.)

Positions, People, and Role Sets

Most everyone fills several positions at the same time. The clergyman, for example, may be a father and husband as well as a minister. The clergywoman may also be a mother and wife. Either may be a trustee on the board of a church-related college, etc. Each position usually involves the fulfilling of several role expectations in relation to more than one person. Thus, as a minister, a person is expected (by many different senders or groups of senders) to play many different roles. All of those who relate to a person in the performance of his ministerial roles are part of the role set of his position as a minister.

The minister's role set would include both the judicatory executive who expects him to emphasize the importance of benevolence giving and the local trustee who expects him to give priority to the building fund so that mortgage payments can be made on time. Also in his role set would be parishioners, vestrymen, elders, deacons, or other church officers, fellow ministers of his judicatory, neighboring clergy, officers of the denomination, community leaders who expect things of him as pastor of "Old First Church," etc.

As has been suggested, a role set relates to only one particular position, such as the position of minister. A given person may have several role sets, each related to one of the positions he occupies. All of those who are related reciprocally to the minister's different roles *as a minister* are part of his role set *as a minister*. Those who relate to him in other positions are parts of the role sets related to *those positions,* but are *not* parts of his role set as a minister. As has been suggested, a clergywoman may also occupy the position of wife and mother. Her husband and children are part of that role set, which of course carries with it various role expectations, rights, and obligations related to being a wife and mother. Technically we may say that only insofar as husband and children may also be parishioners are they part of her role set as a minister. In that case they are part of *two* role sets related to one woman.

The clergyman, therefore, like anyone else, has multiple roles, some related to his position as a minister, others related to his position as a husband or to his position as a father, and still others related to other positions he may occupy. In this work, we shall deal only with the minister's role set related to his position as a minister, and not with role sets related to other positions he may occupy. Thus, we will not try to deal with such questions as the conflicts ministers may face as persons in reconciling the expectations of their families with those of their parish, although such conflicts may be very important indeed, particularly for the younger clergyman who may tend to neglect his family in response to the demands of the parish.

Of course, to try to separate the wife from the clergyman's role set may be a somewhat arbitrary and artificial distinction, since ministers' wives play such important parts in the work of their husbands. She is in various ways inseparable from his role set as a minister. As will be seen, the pastor's wife is the one person whose judgment and approval many ministers value most, and in studies of ministers who have left the pastorate, there is some evidence that wife-related reasons are high on the list. Mills concludes (101:77), "It can be said that the husband role of the minister is, so far as his career decisions are considered, one of the most formative and influential of his role relationships." Similar data is not available on the effect of husbands on the career decisions of their minister wives, but one would assume there might be a similar close relationship.

Role Conflict

The idea of role conflict has already been implicit in what has been said about the minister's role set, and has been illustrated in the varying expectations of judicatory executive and local trustee. It is conceivable that the benevolence-promotion expectations of the judicatory executive might not conflict with the building fund promotion expectations of the local trustee. But to the extent that one expectation makes the other more difficult to fulfill, the minister would experience role conflict.

Role conflict occurs when two or more role expectations interfere with each other or contradict one another altogether. In a mild role conflict, the fulfilling of one expectation may merely make it difficult to fulfill another. In a serious conflict, the compliance with one expectation may make it completely impossible to comply with another.

There are many ways in which conflicts arise in the minister's role expectations. As has been indicated, his role set is made up of a relatively large number of people with diverse backgrounds, convictions, positions, and special interests. The several roles he is expected to play demand an incredibly wide range of skills and require an ability to move from one to another in rather rapid succession. It is no wonder that the minister must often deal with role conflict and ambiguity!

But he is not alone in facing such conflict. Kahn reports that only one sixth of the labor force in the United States is free of job tension. Many experience tensions of such severity that they are costly to both worker and employer. Of male salaried workers, 48 percent report that *occasionally* they are caught between conflicting expectations of those with whom they work, 15 percent indicate that this is *often* a serious problem for them, and 39 percent say they are *sometimes* disturbed with the thought that they may not be able to satisfy these conflicting demands. (76:55, 57.)

So the minister is not alone—but his role problems are often more severe than the average worker's. As will be shown, there are many reasons for this, including the wide range of roles he must play in a position of high visibility, the intensity of some role pressures on him, and the almost complete identity between his self-image and the roles he plays.

Role Ambiguity

When the expectations of others are unclear or confusing, the focal person experiences role ambiguity. The less accurate the information a minister has regarding the roles he is expected to play, the greater will be the ambiguity of his roles. The more accurate his information regarding expectations, the greater his clarity of roles. (76:73.)

There are many possible reasons for role ambiguity. Adequate information on role expectations may not exist. It may exist but not be available to the person who needs it. There may be problems in communication where contradictory messages are being transmitted by role senders who themselves are uncertain what they ought to expect of the focal person. Confusion produces more confusion. In some cases senders may disagree among themselves and thus send contradictory signals. (123.)

Rapid change in society or in an organization may generate confusion in the role expectations of both senders and receiver. Thus much of the role ambiguity among clergy today may be related to the almost cataclysmic changes that are taking place in society and in the reorientation of the church to its calling in the world. As we have noted, there is evidence of considerable confusion among the clergy today. Leiffer's survey (88) found about three quarters of all ministers agreeing with both of the following statements:

"The ministry of today is marked by a sense of confusion and uncertainty about theological verities." (Range from 62.5 percent to 82.0 percent.)

"Changing conceptions of the church's mission have greatly altered the task which confronts the minister." (Range from 57.8 percent to 81.7 percent.)

The layman also is confused. Hadden (61) suggests that this is because of the heterogeneity of clergymen and of the wide range of activities in which they engage (from civil rights activist, to "psychiatrist," to slaves of a church calendar, or executive secretary of the chamber of commerce). No longer does the minister fit a stereotype or affirm a "holy posture," and many laymen have only minimum formal contacts with him, anyway. He uses traditional language but fills it with new meanings that further confuse his parishioners.

Another very important cause of role ambiguity arises from a misunderstanding on the part of the role performer of what the role sender expects of him. Since role-sending and role-receiving are in reality parts of a process of communication, we must keep in mind that the focal person may not understand what was intended by the sender, even though he thinks the message is clear. He will act, however, on the basis of what he understands, rather than on what was intended. (77.)

The importance of this, of course, lies in the fact that sometimes when there appears to be a role conflict, there may actually be no conflict at all. The role performer may simply have misunderstood the expectations of one or more of his role senders. As will be seen later, this has an important bearing on possible solutions to role conflict situations, especially for the clergy.

Figure A illustrates several types of relation between role ambiguity and role conflict. Note that cells 1 and 2 are characterized by ambi-

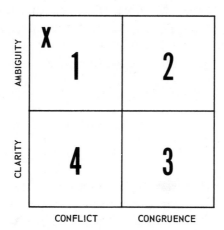

Figure A   RELATIONSHIP BETWEEN
ROLE AMBIGUITY AND ROLE CONFLICT

guity. The minister is not certain what is expected of him. Cells 3 and 4, on the other hand, are characterized by clarity of expectations. When a situation falls within cell 3, there is clear congruence in role expectations. No problem! When it falls within cell 4, there is clear conflict. The lines are plainly drawn, and conflict management becomes the important skill. However, in situations that fall into cells 1 or 2, one cannot be certain how much conflict actually exists because of the ambiguity in the situation. Clarification of role expectations is then the initial task.

Effects of Role Conflict or Ambiguity

Both role conflict and role ambiguity have debilitating effects on the focal person. Kahn and his colleagues have shown that conflict and ambiguity produce a relatively high level of job-related tension, are associated with low job satisfaction and with low self-confidence.

Role ambiguity also results in a sense of futility. Where ambiguity and conflict are both high (as indicated by the "X" mark in the upper left hand corner of cell 1), tension is also high, although the stress is not significantly greater than for ambiguity or conflict alone.

Role conflicts are likely to be most harmful when role senders are very close to the focal person; are dependent upon him; have high power over him; and exert high pressure on him. Most, if not all, of these conditions prevail in the relationships of many pastors to their church officers. Kahn (76) found that when conflict occurs under these conditions, the typical response of most people is to withdraw either behaviorally or psychologically. This may relieve the stress temporarily, but in the long run withdrawal is likely to prove self-defeating, since it leaves the conflict unresolved and, as we shall see, often causes a series of other related conflicts.

Stress in the Ministry

Recent research makes clear that it is quite common for parish clergy to experience stress in connection with their work. Of 4,908 ministers in 21 Protestant denominations, 75 percent reported one or more periods of "major stress" in their careers. Two thirds of these periods involved stress that was characterized as "severe." Two times out of three the source of the stress was identified with the minister's work in the local church. "Almost 30% of all ministers specify this as growing out of personal or ideological conflict with parishioners. Eighteen percent also report frustration, overwork, or lack of achievement as stress-producing, and another 19% describe conflict within the congregation, financial or community troubles of the church, or staff problems as sources." (106:54.)

While all of this stress is obviously not related to role conflict or ambiguity, it appears that much of it may be. It is clear, therefore, that we are not dealing here with a matter of light importance. The morale and the effectiveness of the clergy are at stake.

Different Kinds of Role Conflict

Finally, it appears helpful for orderly review of the role conflicts of the minister to group them according to common characteristics.

Edgar Mills (105:13–15) suggests that in the light of role theory there are three categories of role conflicts that apply to the clergyman: (a) conflicts involving external obligations (such as the priest who is "caught in a cross fire of the essential bureaucratic norms of his superiors, the professional norms of his peers, and the popular norms of his lay clientele"); (b) conflicts between internalized norms, and pressures in the external situation (such as the conflicts a minister feels between the essential tasks of ministry and the many unimportant things which preempt his time); and (c) internalized conflicts (resulting from the minister's appropriating for himself mutually incompatible values and expectations).

These will now be dealt with, one by one, in Chapters 2, 3, and 4.

CHAPTER 2

Conflicts
Among External Expectations

In the pure sense, all role conflicts arise from incompatible *external* expectations. Senders outside oneself are responsible for the clashing norms. However, role receivers, or focal persons, develop role expectations for themselves that must be related to the expectations of others. When these clash, there is an *internal-external* role conflict. In addition, self-expectations sometimes are incompatible with other self-expectations, producing *internalized* role conflicts. These distinctions are helpful in providing a conceptual framework within which to study the role conflicts of the clergy. Operationally, of course, the difference between them is more difficult to distinguish than the framework might seem to imply.

This chapter deals with the fundamental form of conflict: role expectations that originate with members of the minister's role set. The other types of role conflict will be considered later.

For the purposes of this book, two types of external role conflict will be considered: those in which the *senders* conflict with one another in their expectations and those in which the *roles* themselves conflict with each other.

1. *Inter-sender conflict* involves incompatible expectations for the same role or group of roles *from different role senders*. The expectations from one role sender may conflict with the expectations of one or more other senders. The minister is caught between their differing expectations. When the local trustee expects promotion of the building fund will have priority and the judicatory

executive expects benevolence giving will have priority, there is an inter-sender conflict.

2. *Inter-role conflict* involves incompatible expectations inherent in *two different roles*, both of which the minister is expected to play. Role senders may all agree on these expectations, but the roles themselves make conflicting demands. The clergyman's roles of scholar and man of action conflict with one another, for example. Sometimes a single role may combine incompatible expectations. We include that here, although technically it might better be called intra-role conflict.

Inter-Sender Conflict

As has been said, inter-sender conflict involves incongruent expectations from two or more members of the minister's role set.

Several authors contrast the expectations of the local parish with those of the denomination. Church leaders and fellow clergy look for certain signs in a pastor's work by which to judge his success. The numbers game in church membership, size of church budget, and giving to the general mission program of the church might be important illustrations. When the pastor thinks of success, he orients his thinking to the denomination. It is those outside his local parish who can be helpful to him when he wants to move to another parish. Success may become an important factor in achieving such a move, especially if it is to a larger congregation with more salary and prestige. In order to reach such a goal he may need to demonstrate certain specialized skills, spend time in synod or district conference committees, serve on denominational boards, and otherwise show that he is a successful minister.

When he thinks of effectiveness in ministering to his people, however, the pastor orients himself to the parish and to a different set of criteria. This may require spending a great deal of time in quiet and unobtrusive labors with individuals or small groups, completely unnoticed by denominational officials and with little to show for it in the statistical columns of the denominational annual reports.

Blizzard's study (17) of 1,111 ministers has shown that the clergyman's images of effectiveness and of success differ considerably at a

True ·

number of points. *Success* requires general ability in performing the functions of a minister and cooperation in denominational programs, whereas *effectiveness* does not. Character is rated relatively low on the success scale, but comes first for effectiveness. Outgoing personality is important for both success and effectiveness, but skill as a pastor-counselor is much more important for effectiveness than for success.

What then will the pastor do? Will he concentrate his energies on doing a solid job in his local parish or will he give priority to activities that demonstrate his success to others in the denomination, and thus ensure his professional advancement? Divergent expectations of important persons in the minister's role set call for choices that affect his allocation of time and style of ministry. Role conflict has important consequences.

Crisis in the Churches

As has been suggested in Chapter 1, an important cause of role conflict can be rapid social and organizational change. Just such a change is taking place in the social fabric of our nation and in the life of our churches. Crucial role conflicts grow out of this.

An important recent study of major proportions covering 7,441 parish clergy and campus ministers of six denominations (American Baptist, American Lutheran, Episcopal, Methodist, Missouri Synod Lutheran, and United Presbyterian) reveals what Hadden calls "the most serious ferment in Christendom since the Protestant Reformation" (61:3). Drawing on a study by Fukuyama (51), and on other studies, for data on the beliefs of the laity, Hadden comes to a number of far-reaching conclusions. Expectations of laity and of clergy are incompatible. (65:5.)

1. He finds a deep *struggle over the purpose or meaning of the church.* Understandings of the church have been developed by clergy without any meaningful participation by the laity. "Today, laity are beginning to realize that something is different, and for many this is a source of gravest concern, for the new image is in sharp conflict with their own concept of the meaning and purpose of the church." (61:5–6.)

2. There is a *crisis of belief*. "Theology has been shaken at the foundation. But again, the laity have largely been left out of this painful struggle to reinterpret the meaning of the Christian theological heritage for contemporary society." (61:6.) Only one of the six denominations approaches a consensus of belief, and there are great differences within and among them. Both clergy and laity are deeply affected.

3. *There is a struggle over authority*. "Clergy have long been vested with authority to run the church as they have seen fit. Today, laity are discovering that they have grave reservations about the way clergy have handled their authority, and the evidences of power struggles are beginning to be apparent." (61:6.)

It is perhaps unfortunate that Hadden's extensive study did not *itself* deal with the difference between the laity and the clergy, so that it would not be necessary for him to make comparisons between his clergy study of *several* denominations and a study of the laity (51) in different congregations of *one* denomination (the United Church of Christ). Nevertheless, the overwhelming evidence he presents is confirmed by widespread recognition of differences such as he identifies. His findings must be taken quite seriously.

The basic lines of conflict may be described as drawn between a social challenge to change, on the one hand, and personal comfort or reassurance in the midst of life's vicissitudes on the other; between the church as an agent of change in the world and the church as a haven from change; between involvement in social-political-economic issues and concentration upon personal religion. The conflict is between centrifugal and centripetal concepts of the church.

For the layman, religion is a source of *comfort* and *help*. He is a consumer of the church's love, rather than a producer. . . .

Herein lies the basis of conflict between clergy and laity: The clergyman's new theology has moved him beyond the four walls of the church to express God's love in concern for the world, while the layman comes into the sanctuary of God to seek comfort and escape from the world. Clergy have come to see the church as an agent that should be challenging the structures of society that lead to injustice in this life, and to utilize the forces of love and political power to bring about a new social order. This development has left the majority of laymen bewildered and resentful.

For them, the church is not an agent of change, but rather a buffer against it. . . .

From the church they draw love and support, which they pay for with cash and consume when they need it. But this church has become a source of increasing frustration. Their comforter is increasingly telling them that the rules have changed and that they are to become producers of love rather than consumers. (62:20.)

One sees this illustrated quite forcibly in attitudes toward race, for example. When asked to name one controversial issue of personal concern that might arise in their parish or community, 66 percent of the priests in a recent Episcopal study mentioned the issue of race. Only 37 percent felt that they could depend upon adequate support on this issue from their vestries, and only 19 percent felt they could expect support from the older members of their congregations. Only 5 percent felt that they would receive *most* support from members of their vestries. In contrast, 6 percent felt that their vestry members would give them *least* support and 5 percent that their bishop would support them least. Least support was expected by 27 percent from the community, 19 percent from older members of their congregations, and 9 percent from community leaders.

In answers from laymen and clergymen, Hadden found agreement as indicated in Table 1.

Table 1   RACIAL ISSUES – A SOURCE OF LAITY-CLERGY CONFLICT

	Percent of Agreement	
	Laity	Clergy
"Negroes would be better off if they would take advantage of the opportunities that have been made available to them rather than spending so much time protesting."	86%	35%
"I am basically sympathetic with Northern ministers and students who have gone to the South to work for civil rights."	37%	64%

Fukuyama (52) found substantial differences between the attitudes of preachers and seminarians on the one hand and laymen on the other, over the right of denominations to issue policy statements on social and economic matters, on praying in the schools, on civil rights, and on federal legislation to ensure nondiscriminatory housing.

Without fear of significant contradiction, one might add to the list of real differences within the church today such issues as war, poverty, the social responsibilities of investors, justice, the self-development of people, boycotting, demonstrations, lobbying, and various other forms of political action. Of course these are questions which divide our whole society. The point is that the church and its leadership are in the midst of the fray. And the fundamental conflicts that exist have arisen not only in the understanding of these social issues, but more importantly, in the understanding of the church's place in them. Such differences make a vigorous impact on clergy role expectations.

One may well pause at this point to remember that the community in which the clergyman serves is also a part of his role set. Community expectations that are not strictly a part of the minister's professional duties constantly demand time and attention.

If, on the one hand, the minister merely decides to serve as "chaplain" of one organization or member of the board of directors of another, he may experience a type of conflict that really involves the setting of priorities and the management of time. However, if he is oriented toward the bringing about of social change and toward the influencing of power structures, he places himself in another arena and invites role conflict of a completely different order. He will then be dealing with deeply emotional issues that may well focus on influential members of his own congregation, with obvious consequences involving rigorous confrontation.

Cleavage Among the Clergy

Although a clear chasm exists between large bodies of the clergy and the laity, it is important to recognize that the lines are not drawn merely between those two groups. The differences that exist among clergy are an equally important part of the picture.

Hadden's thesis is that the more "liberal and innovative" ministers have systematically entered and saturated the nonparish church positions, serving as campus ministers and church executives. Younger clergy also fall into that category, but all clergy do not.

Leiffer's study (88) confirms that younger ministers are more action-oriented and especially those who are under 30 are much more radical than those who are older. Parish ministers are increasingly conservative with age, and can be distinguished by age groupings. Protestant ministers serving congregations fall into three groups: those under 30; those who are 35 to 54; and those over 55. In the case of Catholic priests, Mills and Koval (106:48) find a particularly acute and sharp polarization between those under 45 and those over 50. Naturally it would be an oversimplification to ascribe all cleavages to this generation gap. The important point is that strong differences in orientation do exist among clergy and that these must be reckoned with by old and young alike.

The polarization that exists among the clergy in many ways resembles the polarization between the political left and the political right in the nation as a whole. Thus, conflicting expectations from two different basic orientations come from relatively large groups of clergy as well as from the laity, further intensifying the withering cross fire of expectation within which ministers labor. Whatever the ideological or theological position the minister affirms, he must deal with rather intense role pressures from these two polarities.

At a later point, the implications of this for role ambiguity will be made clear. At the moment, however, it may be helpful to look at significant invisible forces that further condition a minister's actions in role conflict situations.

Clergy Reference Groups

In understanding inter-sender role conflicts one must recognize some of the centers of power that affect the minister's decisions and the peculiar characteristics of his identifications with valued groups or individuals. The minister is a professional who usually enters the ministry with a sense of divine imperative. "He, more than any other professional, is bound to his calling by an ultimate commitment. At the same time, he is a professional whose clients are often his employers." (105:13.) Thus he may have several different points of reference as justification for his actions. He may feel deeply that God is his ultimate authority. Yet the local church, in congregational polity, may hold the final power over his continued employment. In the presbyterian churches, his ministerial colleagues in presbytery hold his professional future in their hands, but the local congregation pays his salary, and the general presbyter or executive has great power. Similarly, in the episcopal forms of government, the bishop and the district superintendent are authority figures of considerable importance. The demands from these different centers of power, when competing with one another, and when set over against the minister's professional autonomy, may produce important role conflicts and confusion. The concept of *reference group* may be helpful in looking at these forces more carefully. Every person identifies his interests, perspectives, or feelings with other significant people who exercise an influence on him, whether or not they are present. (123.) The way in which a focal person performs his role may be greatly influenced by such a reference group or "symbolic audience." Though not physically present, it is used to evaluate and compare role performance.

In view of the different forces that have just been suggested, one can readily imagine that while the minister is insisting on a point with his board, he is doing so not strictly as a lone individual. The ministerial colleagues of his judicatory may be "looking over his shoulder." He knows that he may be held accountable to them for the stand he takes or fails to take. Conversely, when he participates in a meeting of his judicatory, he will be aware of other reference groups—his board, or women's association, or young adult group, etc. In a sense, they also are watching every important move he makes.

The fact that the minister must look two ways—one way when he is with his church officers and one way when he is with his ministerial colleagues—means he is more likely to be placed in conflict situations. Kahn found that "positions located near the skin or boundary of the organization were likely to be conflict-ridden" (77:192). Also, "living near an intra-organization boundary—for example, serving as liaison between two or more departments—revealed many of the same effects, but to a lesser degree." To the extent that the minister represents the church in the community or otherwise serves as a bridge or channel of communication, he is put in a similar area of potential stress.

Denominational Differences

There appears to be a denominational difference in the reference group that is most important to clergymen. When asked regarding those whose praise they valued in their ministry, 250 United Church of Christ pastors most frequently placed high value on the praise of their wives, followed in order by lay leaders, close friends not included elsewhere in the list, and other church staff (74:182). Interestingly, a study of United Presbyterian pastors who moved from one parish to another (101:123) shows similar results, although the number of pastors studied was only 14. When asked those whose approval they valued most, their order of preference was wife, session, closest friend, and denominational leader. In contrast with these two studies, a third study, done by The Episcopal Church (43, Report 5:19-21) with 970 parish priests, found that rectors ranked those whose judgment concerning their work they would consider most valuable in the following order: bishop, vestry, congregation, wife, fellow clergy. Associates and curates, on the other hand, listed fellow clergy first, then bishop, vestry, and congregation. (See Table 2 for a comparison of these studies.)

It is possible that the difference between these studies grows out of the questions asked. The first two deal with "praise" and "approval," and the third deals with "judgment" concerning the work of the minister. These findings, however, suggest that pastors under the Episcopal form of government tend to look first either to their bishop or to fellow clergy, whereas those in Congregational and Reformed churches tend to depend heavily on their wives and on local church leadership. The former hypothesis seems to be consistent with the study by Glock and Ringer (57) of Episcopal clergy and laymen of 234 congregations, which found that ministers tend to identify with church policy, especially on controversial issues. Thus they differed least with laymen when church policy was equivocal, and they differed most with laymen when it was partisan.

Bennett (14), whose experience has been heavily concentrated in The Episcopal Church, claims that "the major reference groups for the minister are not those provided by the laity, but rather are those composed of fellow professionals who are central in power, authority, and decision-making structures of his denomination."

Interestingly, a still different pattern emerged from a study of Lutheran ministers by Ross Scherer (124). Nine ministerial problem situations were described to ministers. They were asked to select one of two alternative solutions. They were then requested to indicate

Table 2

MINISTERS' REFERENCE GROUPS FOR SEVERAL DENOMINATIONS

Rank given to reference person	Mills (101) United Presbyterian Church		Jud (74) United Church of Christ	Episcopal (43) The Episcopal Church			
	Pastor	Executive	Pastor	Rector	Associate	Curate	Vicar
1.	Wife	Session	Wife	Bishop	Fellow clergy	Fellow clergy	Bishop
2.	Session	Wife	Lay leaders	Vestry	Congregation	Bishop	Congregation
3.	Closest friend	Denominational leader	Close friends	Congregation	Bishop	Vestry	Wife
4.	Denominational leader	Nearby pastor	Other church staff	Wife	Vestry	Congregation	Vestry
5.	Nearby pastor	Trustees	Denominational executive	Fellow clergy	Wife	Other	Fellow clergy
6.	Seminary professor	Seminary professor	Fellow UCC pastors	Other	Other	Wife	Other
7.	Trustees	Closest friend	Fellow pastors same community	God	God	God	God

"what they thought a series of six sets of reference persons might expect them to do." Their own solutions were most closely related to what they thought their wives and children might expect of them. Then came "favorite professor at seminary," "fellow conference clergy," and "nonmember community leaders." Most distantly related to their own solutions were the perceived expectations of "district church officials" and their own "lay officers."

Inter-Role Conflict

Among the various roles that ministers are expected to play there are inherent conflicts which it will be helpful to understand. These inter-role conflicts are not always obvious ones. Some roles, for example, like those of preacher and pastor-counselor are so familiar to everyone that the conflicts between them are not readily recognized. They do exist, however, at least as these roles are generally practiced.

Blizzard's analysis (19) of role conflicts in the urban ministry may be used for illustration, since his description appears to be applicable to the work of ministers wherever they serve.

Table 3 lists in parallel columns some of the styles, abilities, and foci of the role of preacher in contrast with the pastor-counselor role. The preacher who develops a facile tongue and a dramatic ability to express himself may become so enamored with his own good ideas

Table 3   INTER-ROLE CONFLICTS OF THE CLERGY
(Based on Samuel Blizzard, 19)

PREACHER	contrasted with	PASTOR-COUNSELOR
Public expression and illustrations	vs.	Private keeping of confidences
Actor; speaker	vs.	Listener; reactor
"Authoritarian" approach	vs.	Permissive approach
Directive	vs.	Nondirective
Idea-centered	vs.	Person-centered
Actor before an audience, speaker	vs.	Interrelator; listener; reactor
Universal principles	vs.	Particular feelings

SCHOLAR	contrasted with	MAN OF ACTION
Contemplative thought	vs.	Program results
Student of ancient truth	vs.	Applier to contemporary situations
Formulator of ideas	vs.	Organizer and administrator
Dealing with concepts	vs.	Dealing with process and people

and his effectiveness as a verbal communicator that he may lose his ability to really listen to a counselee. To spice his sermons, the preacher is always in need of dramatic illustrations. If he is not very careful, he may violate the confidence of the counseling room, or at least give the impression he is doing so. If he carries a didactic or authoritarian approach into the counseling room, he may be overly directive when he should instead be helping someone to make her own decisions. Preaching to the counselee may satisfy the minister's ego, as he recognizes how keen his insights are and how apt his illustration, but this may not really help the client in the solution of his problems.

Traditionally, the minister is a scholar as well as a man of action. As Table 3 suggests, it takes a rare person indeed to be equally at home in decisive administration and in scholarly contemplation. Yet almost every congregation expects both of its minister.

Fichter (45), in his analysis of religion as an occupation, identifies several other inter-role conflicts. While two of them depend somewhat upon the theological and personality orientation of a particular minister, it may prove helpful to summarize and comment on them here. In a few words, they may be characterized by conflicts between (*a*) the apostolate and sanctification; (*b*) abasement and ambition; and (*c*) generalized pastoral activity and specialized professional competence.

The *apostolate* demands an active life of service to the world. Its fulfillment calls for an outer-directed involvement in the issues of life. In contrast, *sanctification* requires devotion of oneself to prayer and contemplation, through inner-directed quiet periods of separation from the constant drumfire of activity. Historically, in the church the tension between these two dimensions of the Christian life has sometimes been resolved by the setting apart of certain orders whose members give their full time to contemplation. However, for those who cannot accept that kind of dichotomy but who recognize the call to both types of religious response, the conflict must be resolved in some more dynamic form of interrelated activity. The secular priest must find a place for both.

Closely allied to these concerns, perhaps, are those which revolve around the expectation that the clergy will be humble and not self-seeking. The man of God must lose his life if he is to find it. At the same time, a minister is expected to give vigorous leadership in developing the congregation's program. Ambition may be frowned upon, yet the setting of goals and striving to meet them is an almost axiomatic ingredient, not only in organizational accomplishment but also in career development.

Some ministers pride themselves on never having sought a position. It is to the initiative of God that they respond. God calls them. They feel, therefore, that they should wait for his guidance rather than presume to plan their own lives. What, we might ask, about planning the program of the church? Does the setting of goals interfere with the guidance of the Holy Spirit? There are times, we suspect, when patient waiting and humble obedience to the will of God become little more than a pious excuse for indolence or an escape from the rigors of the unknown and the untried.

In Chapter 5, the complexity of clergy roles will be described. At this juncture, we simply recognize the inherent conflict between the expectation that a pastor is to respond (at one and the same time) as a generalist to a very broad range of needs, and as a specialist in Bible, or theology, or counseling, or administration, or whatever other area of competence is seen by a particular congregation to be of top priority. Fichter points out that the frustration of a generalized ministry without fixed schedules and with multifarious unstructured duties is particularly demoralizing to the young priest "who has been brought up in a culture where technical competence of highly specialized work is greatly valued" (45:159).

From the perspective of role conflict, the young priest's dilemma has two possible explanations. If it arises basically from two different expectations of people in his role set, he is experiencing an external role conflict. If, however, as may be more likely, the conflict is between the young priest's image of the ministry and the reality he encounters in its practice, his frustration would more properly be characterized as an internal-external role conflict. This form of role conflict will be discussed in Chapter 3.

CHAPTER 3

Internal-External Role Conflict

The cross fire of role conflicts that is perhaps the most intense for many ministers is the conflict between the person they understand themselves to be and the role they feel required to play. Katz and Kahn (77) refer to this type of conflict as a "person-role" conflict in which "role requirements violate the needs, values or capacities of the focal person." As can readily be imagined, this may be one of the most painful types of conflict because ministers visualize themselves especially as men of integrity. To live a lie by fulfilling expectations they believe to be unimportant or untrue to themselves is to violate this sense of integrity and to cut the nerve of personal identity.

Role Conflict or Hypocrisy?

Perhaps in its most extreme form, the person-role conflict may be seen when the minister finds that he has radically changed his basic convictions about reality. In the midst of a crisis in his own faith, he feels the pressure somehow to continue preaching and comforting and giving assurance to his parishioners as though he himself is some kind of Gibraltar. He may have been called by a particular congregation because they felt that his theology was congenial with theirs. Meanwhile, he has been growing in his understanding of the faith to a point beyond which they are prepared to go. He then faces the necessity either of quietly moving to another parish that believes more nearly as he does (if that is possible), of making an open break and leaving the ministry altogether, or of compromising with his own convictions in order to fulfill the psychological contract into which he entered when he accepted the call. These alternatives are not easy ones, especially when one realizes (*a*) that it is almost impossible for ministers in certain situations to receive a call from another congregation; (*b*) how traumatic it can be to leave a calling in which one's "personal and occupational identities are necessarily linked to his religious identity, so that all three stand or fall together" (105:13); and (*c*) that it is hypocrisy to compromise one's convictions. This is seen by the man of integrity as the greatest of all sins.

Of course, many of the internal-external role conflicts are not of such a severe nature as this, but they are nonetheless important. The same concern for integrity, the same sense of identity, and the same insistence on divine imperative that accompanies a "calling" to the ministry operate in many areas of person-role conflict. It is of great importance to an understanding of clergy in the cross fire that these dynamics be clearly understood.

A good deal of the research into the role of the clergyman that has been done in the last ten years in some way deals with the different dimensions of (*a*) the importance he attaches to each of his roles (involving his ideal for the ministry); (*b*) how he divides his time among them; (*c*) which roles he most enjoys; (*d*) how his ideals relate to the values and expectations of the laity in his congregation; and (*e*) how satisfied he is in filling his different roles (to what extent he is measuring up to his own standards).

Upside-down Priorities

In Blizzard's classic study (16), 690 clergymen were asked to rate six practitioner roles from three perspectives: importance, effectiveness, and enjoyment. These ratings, in turn, were compared with a careful time study of the activities of 480 rural and urban ministers. The results are shown in Table 4.

The most notable conclusion from this study is the marked discrepancy between the amount of time spent in administration (more than on any other activity) and the *low* importance ascribed to it (least important of all activities). Ministers did not enjoy administration very much, and felt they were not very effective in it. The frustration that is suggested by such a disparity seems to be borne out by almost

Table 4   RANK ORDER OF SELF-RATINGS BY CLERGYMEN
                        (Based on Blizzard, 16; Jud, 74:72)

ROLE	IMPORTANCE	EFFECTIVENESS	ENJOYMENT	TIME SPENT
Preacher	1	1	2	3
Pastor	2	2	1	2
Priest	3	4	4	4
Teacher	4	3	3	6
Organizer	5	6	6	5
Administrator	6	5	5	1

every study that is made and by most writing on the subject. Clergy-men, on the whole, do not like their organizational and administrative responsibilities, believe that these duties are not important, and feel they do not do such things well, yet find themselves spending more time in them than in anything else. This is a profound role conflict that must be looked at more carefully below.

The recent Episcopal study (43; see Table 5) confirmed this finding, although the activities used were much more numerous than those in Blizzard's study. Parish priests were asked to check their five most important activities and five least important. Table 5 gives a

Table 5   EPISCOPAL STUDY OF THE CLERGY (43)

ACTIVITY	IMPORTANCE	ENJOYMENT	TIME SPENT		
			Rank	Hours	%
Regular Sunday services	1	1	4.5#	4.7	7.1
Counseling	2	3	10	3.3	4.9
Pastoral calls for a cause	3	5	6	4.3	6.5
Actual teaching	4	4	11	2.8	4.2
Visits to hospitals and institutions	5	9	9	3.4	5.1
Personal prayer and meditation	6	6	12	2.7	4.1
Sermon preparation	7	*3	7	4.0	6.0
Reading and study	8	2	4.5#	4.7	7.1
Regular weekday services	9	7	15	1.5	2.2
Administration	10 (−3)	−7	1	10.8	16.2
ACTIVITIES NOT ON ABOVE LIST IN TOP 10 RANKS FOR TIME SPENT					
Church organizations	13 (−4)	−2	2	5.5	8.3
Diocese-sponsored activities	14 (−6)	−1	3	4.9	7.3
Social visits	12 (−5)	*1	8	3.8	5.7

− Rank order on list of activities considered *least* important or *least* liked.

* Activities *generally liked* (i.e., not on either most liked or least liked list.)

In line with common practice, ties in rank order between two items are indicated by 4.5 (halfway between rank 4 and rank 5).

summary of the rank order of importance, enjoyment, and time spent by these clergymen (the latter on the basis of a diary of time actually spent).

Again, administration takes *most time*. It is ranked tenth among activities considered most important, but, even more significantly, it comes third on the list of activities that are *least important* and seventh on the list of activities that are *least enjoyed*. Only "national church activities" and "other secular work" are considered less important. We should note also that "working with church organizations" and "diocese-sponsored activities" were the two activities enjoyed least of all and were considered very unimportant.

Attenuated Scholar

Another conflict is seen between intellectual activities. Reading and study rank second in enjoyment but between fourth and fifth in time spent. Sermon preparation ranks third in enjoyment but seventh in time spent. The clergyman would rather work with ideas in the study than with organizations in the parish, in the diocese, and in the denomination.

Blizzard's study of urban ministers found them spending 27 minutes a day in general intellectual activities and 38 minutes a day in sermon preparation. Yet their role models were mostly scholars and authors. "When they were asked to name any persons whom they admire or who have greatly influenced the way they think and act as a minister, one-half mentioned well-known religious authors. They have a scholar image of their mentors." (19.) Imagine a scholar or author limiting himself to a little over an hour a day in the study! What a conflict he would have between his own expectations and those imposed by his work! It is no wonder that ministers are frustrated with administration!

What Comes First?

The Episcopal study found the following. (*a*) Of the time that a parish minister spends in parish activities, 62 percent is concerned with the five activities he liked *least*: administration, church organizations, diocese-sponsored meetings, vestry meetings, national church activities. (*b*) The five activities that are *liked most* and considered *most important* (regular Sunday services, counseling, pastoral calls for a cause, actual teaching, visits to hospitals and institutions) take up *less time* in the average workweek (18.5 hours) than those five activities (national church activities, other secular work, administration, church organizations, social visits) which are viewed as *least important* (22.1 hours).

A comparison of Blizzard's study with several other studies made since then suggests the possibility that there may be some denominational differences in role priorities as seen by the clergy. Episcopal clergymen apparently give somewhat higher priority to the priestly functions of conducting worship services. This emerges both from the Episcopal study and from that done by Coates and Kistler (30). Methodists, on the other hand, may give somewhat greater emphasis to pastoral calling and counseling. At least when one combines these two categories in Leiffer's (88) work, it would appear that way. Comparisons are a little difficult to make, since different categories were used in the two inquiries. Blizzard includes both pastoral visitation and counseling in one role. Methodist clergymen, when asked to indicate their three most important tasks, mentioned preaching and worship 821 times, pastoral visitation 825 times, and counseling 425 times.

Roman Catholic priests may spend somewhat more time in personal development (reading, preparation, and prayer) than do clergy of other denominations. At least Schneider and Hall's (125) analysis of the way priests spend their time suggests this. Administration takes 2.2 hours per day; parochial activities (such as the various priestly functions, sick calls, and parish meetings) 2.15 hours; personal development 2.05 hours; community development 1.9 hours; and other activities 2.7 hours per day.

In a study by Chamberlain each minister was asked to record actual communication that took place between himself and others on one weekday and one Sunday. These records were analyzed for contents, means, motives, and networks of personal communication. Chamberlain concluded that the major role of the minister is that of pastor, "with the role of administrator a close competitor." Ministers tend to avoid administrative functions and prefer pastoral activities, whereas their people tend to call on them for "administrative rather than for pastoral services." These ministers gave one fourth of their time to committees and group activities of various kinds giving "prominence to the organizational role, a role in which the minister is not well adjusted, and lacks strategy." (28.)

The Administrative Dilemma

It seems clear that the minister feels himself caught in the cross fire between the intellectual activity and pastoral work that he *wants* to do and the administrative and organizational work that he *must* do. As Dittes suggests, this dilemma affects not only the amount of time he spends on each activity but the way in which he does everything. "This conflict, between two different styles of functioning, saps away his sense of vocational integrity and personal fulfillment. Instead of being concerned about persons for their sake, and instead of putting himself in their service, he finds himself treating them in relation to his purposes and the institution's. The I-Thou relation he intends becomes contradicted by the I-It relation he finds himself pursuing." (36:104–105.) What are the roots of this dilemma?

Colwell (31) believes that the administrator and organizer roles are built into the institutional structure, and pressures for conformity to them are inevitable. He suggests that denominational officials (in the Congregational Christian Church) are least committed to the roles of pastor, preacher, priest, and teacher, and hold doctrines of the church that legitimize the function of parish ministers in roles approximating that of a business executive. He finds that the minister who resists conformity to congregational administrative-organizational expectations during the first year of his pastorate, and whose resistance increases to twice the intensity during the third and fourth years, finally capitulates during the fifth year and beyond. Apparently, therefore, by the fifth year, ministers spend more time in the administrative and organizer functions either "because they really want to, or because maintenance of the institutional structure seems to require it."

Although Colwell makes a case for the institutional pressures as being determinative, we should not ignore the other alternative. It is possible, as Dittes suggests, that in spite of what he says, the minister is really *attracted to* administrative tasks because they are more tangible and provide more evidence of concrete achievement than is otherwise possible in working with ideas and people. Administration provides "relieving surcease from the more demanding tasks." Expression of dislike for administration may be a scapegoat for other problems or a form of self-denigration. "When we get restive with these administrative activities and keep saying we want to discard them so that we can get on with the real ministry, how often are we mostly saying, 'If I am doing it, it cannot be very important or effective.'" (36:114–115.)

Conversely, it is possible that administration actually gives the minister a feeling of importance and an opportunity to control the destinies of the congregation and of the people in it. However, because the servant image is so deeply ingrained in his consciousness, he cannot allow himself to acknowledge the enjoyment he finds in it. Feelings of ambition and desire for power must be denied. Many pastors find it difficult even to talk about success. It violates their sensitivities. As dedicated servants of the Lord, they may even fall into the "Elijah trap," feeling that God's mission is completely dependent on their faithfulness. Yet "he who is first must be last," and the traditional roles of the pastor do not include administration and organization, so he cannot admit, even to himself, that he is really spending his time the way he unconsciously wants to spend it, in administration! In short, his administrative dilemma may be of his own creation.

Self-Image: "Minister"

How can we explain some of the internal-external conflicts we have summarized? If, as Super (132) has shown, occupational development is best described as a process of developing and implementing a self-image, we may find our clues in the process by which the minister has related his growing self-image to what he knows of the ministry. The hypothesis would be that conflicts will emerge in the pastorate to the extent that the minister's self-image has been shaped in relation to an unrealistic image of the role demands of the clergyman.

The role image of the clergyman which a young minister brings with him to his first parish developed through many experiences over his whole lifetime. As a boy growing into adolescence, he knew one or more ministers and through his interaction with them got a picture of what a minister is and does. He saw the preacher in the pulpit, the teacher in the church school class, the pastor in the home. The traditional roles of minister were demonstrated in the lives of the ministers he knew. As he reflected on his abilities, interests, and personal needs, he found the image of a clergyman compatible with the person he was. Perhaps he had an opportunity to speak from the pulpit on youth Sunday, or to take a leadership part in a summer conference. It is not likely that he had too many contacts with the minister in his administrative capacities. He probably never attended a board or judicatory meeting except when he was accepted as a candidate for the ministry. He did not see the pastor's struggles to organize the every member canvass, or recruit teachers for the church school. He did not type the church bulletin, operate the mimeograph machine, or spend endless hours in denominational committee meetings. Nor was he attracted to the ministry by a desire for institutional leadership so much as by the intention of helping people to effect changes in their individual lives or in the social structures that affect them. (74.)

Seminary only served to confirm prior traditional images. The seminarian was expected to be a religious scholar. "Practical theology" emphasized an ability to express himself from the pulpit, and to do pastoral calling, or even counseling, and to perform his various priestly functions. He spent more time learning Hebrew or Greek than in understanding group process. His role model was the scholar, especially if he was a good student. Eggleston found, in a study of seminarians and professors, that there was "no significant difference in the way faculty priests and seminarians perceived the role of priest" (42). That seminaries influence the students' expectations of the ministry seems emphasized by the study of Kendall, who found that ministerial stereotypes among students were closer to agreement the longer they were in seminary.

In describing this socialization process, one must be quick to recognize that it is an oversimplification. That scholarly and other traditional images of the ministry are reinforced in many seminaries seems clear. But it is at least equally certain that many seminarians acquire or develop a theology of the church and of involvement in the world that can lead to expectations conflicting with those of their parishioners, as described in Chapter 2. Some reject the traditional clergy roles, forsake the idea of the pastorate altogether, and choose secular employment as their avenue of ministry. Others acquire a style of parish ministry that conflicts with traditional expectations and leads to the charge that seminaries are "turning out radicals."

At the same time, the extent of the seminary emphasis on the traditional roles is illustrated by the report of the Special Committee on Theological Education of The Episcopal Church, entitled *Ministry for Tomorrow* (121). The membership of the committee included such prestigious names as Nathan M. Pusey, Gordon Allport, Charles L. Taylor, James F. Hopewell, and Herman Morse. Though the study, published as recently as 1967, recognizes the administrative dilemma, with appropriate references to Blizzard's study and a quotation from a young minister, its role analysis comes under a section on the "Traditional Functions of the Parish Ministry," in which there is no mention whatever of the administrative and organizational expectations of congregations and denominational executives. In many ways it is a very progressive report. The committee strongly recommends supervised field education, clinical training, practice in the work of ministering, and "the use of case method and/or process method of teaching wherever suitable." Yet no specific mention is made of the need to give major effort in the development of such skills as those involved in group work, sensitivity training, conflict management, management theory, etc. Perhaps these are present by implication, but the administrative dimension does not seem to this author to be given an emphasis commensurate with the time that seminary graduates will be expected to spend in it.

Certainly the committee's report is a step in the right direction, but seminaries must go even farther. In their study of ex-pastors, the United Church of Christ found that pastors agreed overwhelmingly with ex-pastors that their seminaries had not prepared them in the practical skills they needed for the pastorate. Specifically they mentioned such skills as "change agentry, clinical training, conflict management, group therapy, leadership training, business administration" (74:23).

In a survey of 1,200 pastors and 1,300 seminarians, Fukuyama (52) found that only 6 percent of the students and 11 percent of the pastors felt that the seminaries are "doing a good job training ministers." By contrast, 32 percent of the students and 22 percent of the pastors felt that "theological education 'needs to be completely overhauled.' "

Similarly, the Episcopal study (43 and 78:3) found that parish priests feel they have been inadequately prepared in several areas (percentages of respondents naming each item are indicated in parentheses): social problems (71 percent); communications (71 percent); Christian education (68 percent); public relations (66 percent); psychology and counseling (65 percent); administration and organization techniques (65 percent); pastoral care (60 percent). Two thirds of the clergy felt they had received inadequate preparation in the administration of the parish. (43:3.) Thirty-seven percent felt they needed more training in group work, counseling, youth work, sensitivity training, and psychology. While one suspects that practitioners in many professions have a similar feeling of being ill-prepared for their practical tasks, the need of ministers for such preparation is nonetheless clear.

In working with over 1,600 ministers from 38 denominations over a period of seven years, Reuel L. Howe was particularly impressed "by the contrast between the certainty of the theological student's preconceptions of the ministry and the veteran minister's confusion about it." He attributes some of this to expectations of the ministry generated in theological training in contrast to the actual conditions encountered in the parish. (72:207.)

As one illustration of this, Howe points to the emphasis in seminaries upon Biblical and theological studies and the use of related terminology. "When they are ejected from this womb of theological coziness, they discover that the world does not operate on the same presuppositions or that it is not motivated by the same orientations." (72:208.)

The Early Parish Years

The study of stress in the ministry (106), cited earlier, discovered that of the 6,195 periods of stress reported by 4,665 ministers, 42 percent took place during the first five years of the pastorate and more than 25 percent were in the first two years. Whereas stress does recur throughout the careers of ministers, much of it comes during the early years and the job-related causes in these early stress periods tend to recur in later periods of stress. Furthermore, ministers tend to repeat the same kinds of steps to resolve their stress when they do recur. It is clear, therefore, that the early parish years are particularly crucial for a minister's effectiveness.

The shock that a young minister experiences in his first pastorate seems to be inversely proportional to the realism of his image of the ministry. Mills's study (101) of 60 ministers who moved from the pastorate found that those who left the parish for secular work (whom he calls "seculars") or for graduate work had experienced many more "unwelcome surprises" in their first parishes than those who moved to another parish ("pastors") or to work as denominational executives. Their greatest disillusionment seemed to be in relation to the church's ability to influence the community and the church's relevance to everyday life. They expressed disappointment with the minister's job, with the responsiveness of the laity, and with personal benefits. The average length of the pastorate for "seculars" was 2.5 years, in contrast with 4.5 years for the "executives" and the "pastors." Thus during the stage of life when most persons are getting established in their careers (132 and 133), the seculars showed a very unstable pattern without longer, settled pastorates. Mills concludes that they "appear never really to have succeeded in the stabilization process" (101).

Unwelcome surprises for the "graduate students" were slightly fewer than for the "seculars," but many of them seem to have chosen the pastorate in the first place as a part of a career plan that saw the pastorate as necessary preparation for teaching.

Mills interprets the sharp differences in the average surprise scores as being principally related to more realistic expectations on the part of the "pastors" and "executives." At the same time, he points out that their scores may have been lower because they were older and had forgotten some of their surprises.

In any case, the point seems to be clear that the socialization of ministerial students and the process of training for the ministry frequently do not provide a realistic picture of the ministry, and the early years in the pastorate must be occupied with necessary shifts in understanding of roles, image of self, and styles of role performance. The Episcopal study (43) supports this. Two thirds of the priests felt that their conception of the role of the parish priest had changed either very much (30 percent) or somewhat (36 percent). The greatest change seems to have been in their understanding of the "duties, activities, and functions" of the priest: 25 percent felt that the change had been in a *negative* direction, 16 percent felt it had been in a *positive* direction, and 22 percent assigned a *neutral* quality to the change.

In a study of "drop-outs" from the parish ministry, Wilson (147) concludes that men leaving the pastorate "tended to have a 'fairly rigid view of what the church *ought to be.*'" When reality did not coincide with this view, they could not adjust to it and so moved on to some other type of work.

During the establishment phase of the clergyman's career the critical question is this: To what extent can he make a successful transition from his early understanding of who he is as a minister to a self-concept that is able to come to terms with the role demands of his situation?

Professional training for the ministry, as for other fields, includes the nurture of a ministerial self-image. As the young minister enters his first pastorate, he seeks to test and confirm this newly-acquired identity. In the course of time, his assertion "I am a minister" must also carry assurance that "I *like* being a minister, I am an *effective* minister, and *others respond* to my ministry." In other words, his experience must demonstrate to him that his self-image is congruent with the ministerial role, that he is doing (or can do) a good job, and that he is accepted as a minister by laymen and fellow ministers. This confirmation by occupational identity is an important part of the developmental task termed by Super (1963) "stabilization in a vocation." (101:144.)

A Self-actualizing Climate

One additional dimension of importance in considering the internal-external role conflicts of the minister is the work climate in which he operates. The professional expects a certain amount of autonomy to carry out his work in relation to goals he considers important. Whether or not a minister actually has such opportunity in any particular situation depends upon the degree to which the role definitions permit it. If they do not, his needs for self-actualization will be thwarted, and his professional expectations will conflict with organizational expectations. This may be of particular importance in multiple staff relationships, but it is applicable to all.

Healthy individuals need the challenge of striving for worthy goals and the corollary sense of competence growing out of achieving such goals through their own efforts. A sense of competence enables one to value himself. Self-esteem, in turn, enables a person to be more open with others, releases psychological energy, and encourages a person to set still higher goals. (10.)

Kurt Lewin has shown that a person can be psychologically successful in a working situation when he himself is allowed to choose goals that challenge him and require his best efforts, when he himself determines the path he will use to reach them, when he sees his goals as meaningful to his self-concept, when he is able to relate them to goals of the organization, and when, by his own evaluation, he has been successful in attaining his objectives. (10 and 125.)

Schneider and Hall applied these principles to an analysis of diocesan priests in Hartford and found that their assignment characteristics, career patterns, and relationships worked against psychological success.

1. "There is little evidence of active choosing on the part of the priest, and little evidence of the system offering any opportunity to choose" (125). Priests have little control over their careers. Promotion from curate to priest takes place on the basis of seniority, often relatively late in career. Fichter says that this may take from five to thirty years. "In the very largest dioceses, recently ordained priests have been advised that they may never reach the pastorate" (45:135). The curate has no control over his assignment and little choice about what duties he will perform, or how he will perform them. He must live with the pastor and other curates. Pastors have somewhat greater choice about how they do their work and more control over the location of their assignments.

2. Curates find that the pastors for whom they work tend to go to one extreme or another. Either they are autocratic or laissez-faire in their leadership. Either they allow little autonomy and supervise too closely or they ignore the curate entirely and abdicate responsibility for his work.

3. Curates feel they are less involved in community activities and personal development than pastors or priests on special assignment, though they consider these activities to be very important.

4. Because adequate performance is difficult to define in the priesthood and because feedback is inadequate, it is difficult for priests to know whether or not they have reached their goal.

The study concludes that assistant pastors do not work under conditions necessary for psychological success in their careers. The conditions for priests are somewhat better, but, the authors say, "one is hard-pressed to think of extant occupational systems of professional personnel with fewer structural opportunities for individual psychological success and growth."

In the light of these findings, it is not strange to find that job satisfaction for priests, as measured with the Job Description Index created by Smith, Kendall, and Hulin (1969), was found to rank below the average for professional men, nor that Catholic clergy experience more stress with greater severity than do Protestant ministers (106:48). "Compared with the professional norms, curates again score extremely low on satisfaction; on satisfaction with their work, supervision, promotion and people, curates rank lower than 85% of the professional people in the norms sample." (125:115–116.) That low satisfaction is related to work environment is shown by the fact that when curates describe their work environment in positive terms, "they also experience positive career outcomes, . . . are more satisfied with their work, their supervision, the other people they come in contact with, and their feeling that their important skills and abilities are being utilized" (125:115–116).

Comparable studies of ministers of Protestant denominations are not available. However, from general knowledge of their work situations, we can state the following propositions regarding conditions for their psychological success:

1. Ministers generally have more choice than priests in their career patterns and there is more possibility of movement in the direction of career goals. Many clergy, however, do have difficulty in moving from undesirable parish assignments when they wish to.

To the extent that this is true, they may face similar frustrations. Many ministers are married and, therefore, do not face the restrictive living arrangements that the unmarried priest must accept.

2. Leadership styles similar to those experienced by curates are most likely to affect assistant or associate pastors in Protestant churches, but pastors may face similar problems when role expectations on the part of church officers or judicatory executives rigidly prescribe or circumscribe their activity and give them little room for creativity in setting their own goals.

3. To the extent that the minister experiences the internal-external role conflicts outlined in this chapter, his opportunities for psychological success will be hampered as are the curate's.

4. The performance of the Protestant minister is as difficult to define or measure as the performance of the priest, and securing adequate feedback is a problem of equal, if not of greater, difficulty for the minister. Part III will consider this in some detail.

CHAPTER 4

Internalized Role Conflicts

Some role conflicts and ambiguities make a lasting impact upon the role receiver. As we have seen, it is the *perceived* incongruity of expectations that affects the minister and that influences his response. It is not mere abstract or impersonal pressures we are discussing here. The minister *himself* is changed by the role pressures he experiences. As expectations are perceived, they may be blocked off and ignored or accepted and acted upon. Those expectations which fit into the receiver's self-concept or present a meaningful challenge to it may be appropriated and internalized. Thus the expectations of others may become the minister's own expectations. Conflict or ambiguity may also be internalized.

As the last in his series of crises, Hadden describes the crisis of identity that comes from the "internalization of the other crises." The rapid change in the social fabric of our nation, the ambiguity in the mission of the church, the flux in values and beliefs, all produce strain in the community of the church. This stress is felt most keenly by ministers because they carry a basic responsibility for those values and their inculcation in others. Furthermore, because the values that are being challenged have to do with ultimate reality, ministers feel the strain acutely.

Occupation and Identity

It is now widely accepted that vocational development involves the establishment and implementation of a self-concept (132). One would expect, therefore, that the minister's self-image would be closely related to his expectations for himself as a minister. Kendall finds that the longer one is in the ministry, the more he identifies his self-image with his concepts of the "typical minister." At the same time, the longer a minister is in service, the more his picture of the "typical minister" differs from the "typical minister" image held by other ministers. In other words, either he *becomes* what he believes a minister to be, or he modifies his belief about ministers in the direction of what he is.

This is really not strange, when one thinks of what happens to most people when their responsibilities are changed radically. With the new job they soon express new points of view and act in ways that are appropriate to their new responsibilities. For example, the pastor who becomes a judicatory executive begins to think and act like an executive rather than a pastor. Lieberman's study illustrates this. Soon after factory workers filled out questionnaires on their attitudes toward unions and management, some were promoted to foremen and others to union stewards. "Upon reassessment of attitudes, new foremen expressed more favorable attitudes toward management, and new union stewards less favorable attitudes. The men endorsed attitudes congruent with their newly acquired statuses." (123:554–555.) Interestingly, those who subsequently returned to the status of worker were found to change their attitudes again, once more appropriate to their roles as workers. Attitudes change as people play different roles. We become what we do.

I Am *a Minister*

As Friedman and Havighurst (49) have pointed out, the higher a worker is in the occupational hierarchy, the more he views his work as a way of life, rather than a way to earn a living. This is true of all professions, but as has been suggested earlier, it is especially true for the clergyman. His self-identity and his roles are almost completely merged. The tradition that thinks of him as a "believer-saint" and as an example to all men sets an impossible expectation before him. Many of the younger clergymen are rebelling against this expectation (88), but one wonders if, even for them, there may not be enough unconscious residue of the old image left to cause internal conflicts between the minister as an "ideal person" and the minister as an ordinary human being. It is conceivable, for example, that clergymen who make a special point of using strong "manly" language are doing so in order to prove to themselves, as to others, that they do not need to conform to the expectation of being a "saint."

In any case, the saintly expectations for the clergy have a strong enough grip on most ministers that Margaretta Bowers finds this to be characteristic of her patients' expectations for themselves. As a psychiatrist, she has treated a number of clergymen. Although her case illustrations come from the priesthood, she makes clear that denominational differences do not affect this "burden of the ideal self-image."

For a priest is a miracle of God's love to us; a man who, through His sacrament of Ordination, becomes *another* Christ with powers that beggar human imagination. . . . Nothing can be greater in this world of ours than a priest. Nothing but God Himself.

A priest is a holy man because he walks before the Face of the all Holy.
A priest understands all things.
A priest forgives all things.
A priest is a man who lives to serve.
A priest is a man who has crucified himself, so that he too may be lifted up and draw all things to Christ.
A priest is a symbol of the Word made flesh.
A priest is the naked sword of God's justice.
A priest is the hand of God's mercy.
A priest is the reflection of God's love.
He teaches God to us. . . . He brings God to us. . . . He represents God to us.

This statement on the nature of priesthood, though put in exalted terms, reflects in a very real sense the clergyman's ideal self-image, and at the same time intimates the staggering demands on his heart and conscience if he is to fulfill it.

The nature of the ministry with the awesome demands it places on the self-image of the individual minister constitutes the most formidable obstacle in the path of clerical psychotherapy. It is an integral part of the priestly self-image that if the minister is sick in his religious life, he should be able to cure himself. And when he finds that the Sacraments do not heal him, and that all of the beneficent services of the Church do not heal him, when he finds himself unable to pray, he feels that this means only one thing—he is bad. He cannot believe that it may just mean that he needs a doctor. It is very, very difficult for the clergy to realize that their religious life can be healthy or sick, and that if sick, it can be exposed to therapeutic intervention in the same way that their bodies can. The idea that if they prayed their spiritual disturbances would disappear is deeply rooted not only in their minds, but in the minds of their congregations. (22:10–12.)

This is indeed a grim picture, and fortunately there seem to be signs of change in these expectations both by parishioners and by the clergy themselves. But there are other aspects of the life of the clergyman that tend to put continual pressure on him in the direction of complete identity between self and role expectations. Of all the professions, that of the minister is most continually under observation by his clients. Many of his role performances are in public, and not infrequently he lives in a manse next door to the church, where even his personal life is likely to be observed. He is expected to respond willingly to any call upon his services at any time of the day or night. His days off are often not respected, and his social life may often be with parishioners. He may never be able to escape the frustrations and anxieties that accumulate during the working day. Thus, he is continually on display. "Role enactment that is observable by a variety of other persons makes the role more vulnerable to positive and negative sanctions from audiences than does role enactment that is restricted from observation." (123:533.) On top of this, the "denial of self" that is so much a part of the servant image may often be imposed on the minister by parishioners who desire his services. To the extent that the servant role is internalized as a demand that the minister places on himself and his family, he will find himself struggling with internal conflicts between legitimate self-interest and the unceasing demands of the parish.

Somehow the "man of God" needs to free himself to be human and to separate his role image from his personal identity sufficiently so that the two are not completely fused. "When an occupational role becomes all that a person is, rather than much that he is, the clergyman has lost touch with his own reality. Then the role hardens into a label shutting off vitality." (11:35–36.)

The "Out There" Is In Here

Beyond the vital question of identity, perhaps the most important point to be made in this chapter is that any of the external role conflicts that arise from the expectations of others may be appropriated by the clergyman as his own somewhere along the way. The conflicts may persist within him even if and when the expectations from others cease altogether. He becomes a "self-sender" of conflicting expectations. (77.) He needs to be aware of this and to determine in a given situation whether the conflict he feels is related to the *real* and *current* expectations of those in his role set or is, in reality, his own conflict, which he continues to project into the working situation.

Take the clergyman's struggle between ministering to the personal needs of parishioners and ministering to the needs of society.

> While in seminary he internalized the truth that the church exists for the sake of the world. The local church is to be "society problem centered." This involves massive amounts of the clergyman's time in the community. At the same time, he has internalized the imperative of being the "shepherd of the flock." He wants to do both and is in serious tension because to do both well is almost impossible for him. (74:120–121.)

A minister with the conflicting self-expectations described here could be in a congregation that clearly expected only one or the other of these alternatives, or had little concern which of them prevailed, and he would still feel role conflict. The struggle is within. Or take the conflict between activities leading to denominational success or to parish effectiveness. These too can be internalized conflicts in the minister. From the church, he has learned "the ethic of self-denial and loving service" (105). From American society he has absorbed the values of competition and achievement. And the struggle is all the stronger because he has learned to repress as inappropriate, as a denial of responsiveness to the Holy Spirit, or even as "sinful pride," the notion that he could have any interest in achievement.

Clergy in particular react strangely: they are highly sensitive to feelings of failure or futility in their present positions, but they often reject attempts to identify "success" in ministry. One reason is that there is very little goal-setting in the ministry, and thus very few criteria which are concrete enough to be useful. A second reason is that advancement patterns in the church allow relatively little feedback of evidence that one is successful. Still a third reason is the subculture of self-denigration in the church: humility is so threatened by success that the latter must be stripped of real content in order to avoid pride and guilt. (102:188–189.)

Or again, after a pastor has overcome the initial shock of discovering that he cannot give as much time to scholarly pursuits as he had hoped in seminary, and after he has discovered the importance of being a man of action as well as a man of contemplation, the struggle between these alternatives can continue within him as he battles the pressures of setting his own priorities for ministry. His people may be perfectly happy to let him establish his own priorities and to be the kind of minister he feels he should be. But now the conflict is within, and he finds it difficult to escape. He is caught in the cross fire of his own expectations!

Internal Crises

As has been suggested, the interplay of one's self-image with the expectations of others and the experiences of ministry leads to a continual testing and modification of the self-image. When the minister's picture of the ideal self, the ideal clergyman, the perceived self, and the perceived expectations of others is sufficiently incongruent, he needs help to work through just who he really is and what he has to contribute, and where. For several years, the Northeast Career Center at Princeton has provided such help to ministers at potential turning points in their careers. Brown (24 and 26) enumerates the major crises that he has identified in dealing with over one thousand clients. All of these deal with one internal conflict or another.

1. The crisis of *Integrity:* the feeling of falseness from a discrepancy between one's beliefs and one's true situation, and one's outer profession or activity.

2. The crisis of *Power:* a feeling that one lacks the authority, recognition, or power to influence a situation, partly at least because of feelings that the church itself is ineffectual.

3. The crisis of *Capacity:* a feeling that one lacks the ability to use the authority or power at his disposal.

4. The crisis of *Failure, or fear of failure.*

5. The crisis of *Destination:* a concern for where the church is going in view of institutional ambiguity.

6. The crisis of *Role:* a concern for how one gets to the destination (including role conflict).

7. The crisis of *Meaning:* a concern for "What does it all add up to?"

Career counseling may help the minister, at almost any stage of his career, to deal with his internal conflicts through discovering more clearly what kind of person he is, what gifts he brings to his calling, and how he may focus his ministry. However, before we move to a consideration of the ways in which a clergyman may clarify role ambiguities or minimize and manage role conflicts, we need to look briefly at the complexity and sheer magnitude of the expectations he seeks to fulfill. This will be the subject of Chapter 5.

Role Flexibility and Overload

So far, the role conflicts and ambiguities of the clergy have been described and illustrated, but no attempt has been made to list the roles themselves. What are the generally accepted functions of the ministry? What do most people expect from a clergyman?

The Tasks of the Ministry

Blizzard's role studies are most widely known and cited. As has been observed, most other more recent studies seem to build on or modify some of the basic work he did. He identified six "practitioner roles" (16), those functional activities which most ministers are expected to perform. Three of these he refers to as *traditional* roles: *preacher, priest,* and *teacher.* One role, *pastor,* is neotraditional, in that the Biblical and theological definition of the shepherding function has been modified by the more modern insights of clinical psychology and counseling. There are two *contemporary* roles: *administrator,* which involves those functions concerned with managing a parish, and *organizer,* which includes the clergyman's leadership in local church associations and community organizations. Blizzard also develops the idea of the clergyman's "integrating roles," which concern his principal purposes in ministry, and his "master role" or that unifying concept of his activity which is distinctive to the profession of the minister. These two concepts will be dealt with in Chapter 7, since they seem to be helpful in suggesting ways in which the minister can manage his role conflicts.

A number of studies have analyzed the common clergy functions.

Some lists have been based on Blizzard's practitioner roles, but others have been derived by factor analysis. In addition to those summarized in Tables 6 and 7, we should mention research by Kolarik (85), Higgins and Dittes (71), Wood (148), Hadden (63), Fichter (45), and "the Episcopal study" (43). Table 6 lists the four major factors

Table 6   COMPONENTS OF FOUR FACTORS OF PRIEST ACTIVITIES
(Schneider and Hall, 125)

1. PAROCHIAL
   Saying Mass in church
   Marriages
   Baptisms
   Funerals
   Religious instructions
   Teaching (non-religious) courses in school
   Visiting the sick
   Parish organization meetings
   Non-marriage counseling

2. ADMINISTRATION
   Supervising lay employees
   Parish administration
   School administration
   Raising funds
   Administering Diocesan affairs
   Supervising priests and/or sisters

3. COMMUNITY INVOLVEMENT
   Ecumenical work
   Community meetings
   Inner-city work
   Attending workshops and conferences
   Saying Mass in homes
   Home visitation
   Being on call outside the rectory
   Motivating the laity to become more active Catholics

4. PERSONAL DEVELOPMENT
   Reading
   Private prayer
   Preparation for duties
   Training (self-improvement)

or statistical clusters of activities engaged in by the Roman Catholic priest. These have been derived by factor analysis. In many ways they are similar to the activities of Protestant clergymen set forth in Table 7. In others they are different. School administration, for example, is much more frequently a part of a pastor's responsibility in the Roman Catholic Church than in most Protestant denominations.

Column (B) of Table 7 shows the functions of the clergyman as derived by Kling (83 and 84) through factor analysis and as revised and grouped by Mills (101:92). The scheme that Mills has used for grouping he adapted from Seward Hiltner. It has the advantage of combining the functional demands of the ministry into three groupings, each of which might also be seen as a perspective on the ministry cutting across other role areas as well. Each grouping requires somewhat different interest patterns and skills.

1. *Communication* as defined here requires working with groups or large audiences in expressing concepts and in motivating response.

Table 7

COMPARISON OF FUNCTIONS OF THE MINISTRY

(A) BLIZZARD	(B) MILLS (derived from Kling and Hiltner)	(C) CHURCH MANPOWER SYSTEM	(D) ASHBROOK	(E) PROPOSED
Preacher	COMMUNICATING ROLES — Priest, preacher, scholar, believer	Preaching	EXPRESSIVE: Preaching	EXPRESSIVE: Preaching
Priest		Worship	Worship	Worship
Teacher	Teacher	Teach children	Teaching	Teaching
		Teach youth		
		Teach adults		
		Evangelism		
		Theology		
		Stewardship		
		Social ministry		Social ministry
	PASTORAL ROLES — Counselor and problem solver	Counseling	Counseling	Counselor and problem solver
		Visiting — crisis		Visiting — crisis
Pastor	Pastoral visitor	Visiting	INSTRUMENTAL: Calling	INSTRUMENTAL: Calling
Organizer	ORGANIZING ROLES — Community and denominational activity	Community leader	Community involvement	Community involvement
	Planner and promoter of church programs		Denominational involvement	Denominational involvement
		Interchurch cooperation	Ecumenical involvement	Ecumenical involvement
Administrator	Administration of church affairs	Administrative leadership	Administration-Organization	Administration-Organization

2. The *pastoral* cluster involves one-to-one relationships or working with couples in face-to-face encounters around the counselees' interests and concerns.

3. The *organizer* roles include the skills of goal-setting, planning, motivating, delegating, and reviewing the institutional program, working with small groups or individuals whose aim is the accomplishing of tasks within the life of the church or community.

The functional listing of ministerial activities from the new Church Manpower System—Table 7, column (C)—was developed jointly by The Episcopal Church, the American Baptist Convention, the Lutheran Church in America, and the National Council of Churches. (91.) It is included here because of its somewhat more detailed breakdown of activities, and because it represents the best common judgment of several denominations on an operational definition for clergy roles. Ministers of these churches who seek the help of their denominations in placement are now expected to indicate their interests and abilities along these lines, and congregations are asked to state their expectations for a new minister in terms of these categories.

Ashbrook's grouping of ministerial tasks, column (D), was used in his study of task satisfaction of clergymen as a means of predicting organizational effectiveness. While it may be argued that the *expressive* and *instrumental* categories used here are more accurately defined as perspectives on the ministry than as logically defensible categories of ministerial tasks, Ashbrook's classification does have a certain advantage. There is a considerable body of evidence showing that ministers tend to contrast those activities which are of the _essence_ of traditional ministry with those which are related to the _maintenance_ of the institution. Ashbrook's classification reflects this. It is true that the minister will inevitably have both instrumental and expressive purposes in the performance of his various role tasks. Yet in this scheme these role tasks are listed within the category that is most likely to predominate in the performance of that task.

We have already examined at some length the feelings of ministers about administration. Ashbrook's "Expressive" and "Instrumental" categories reflect this concern and organize the functions accordingly:

Expressive purposes are defined as those which establish and enhance the manifestly religious purpose of the church—namely, the increase of "love of God and neighbor." That would include such tasks as leading a worship service or such behavior as being concerned with the well-being of members. Expressive purposes have no utilitarian intent beyond that of giving expression to what constitutes the raison d'être of the organization.

Instrumental means are defined as those which create and maintain the organization and are the methods by which the purpose is expressed. That would include such tasks as administering the institution or such behavior as stressing the carrying out of specific responsibilities. Instrumental means are designed to sustain the organization in order that it may carry out its purposes. (12:6.)

One should note, in examining Ashbrook's categories, that a distinction is made (as with numerous other classifications) between "counseling," which is defined as "face-to-face pastoral work with individuals," and "calling," which is "contacting individuals to relate the church to them and them to the church."

For purposes of the balance of the discussion in this book, Ashbrook's distinction between *expressive* and *instrumental* tasks is used, but his breakdown of functions is altered somewhat, as proposed in Table 7, column (E). Note that the activity of "social ministry" has been added from the Church Manpower System categories, because this is an area of increasing emphasis by many clergymen. As has been indicated, this is also a point of conflict between different members of the minister's role set. Finally, the proposed classification also distinguishes between the supportive type of face-to-face pastoral activity that the Church Manpower System calls "visiting—crisis," and "counseling," which involves a more formal setting in which to help persons deal with problems or make decisions. "Visiting—crisis" is defined as "visiting people in the midst of crisis; e.g., death, sickness, trauma or other significant points in individual lives."

Versatility—Virtue or Mandate?

There are few professions, if any, that demand as broad a range of different skills and styles of action as the ministry. Analysis of the wide range of incongruent expectations that the clergyman experiences has already made this clear. Now we will look more specifically, and somewhat more systematically, at some of the dimensions of these demands. Table 8 examines several different variables that affect the manner in which a clergyman performs the expressive and instrumental roles listed in the left-hand column. In looking at these variables, we will remind ourselves of many things already said in earlier chapters.

First, in any role performance, we can identify what aspect of the clergyman's work system is being dealt with. The minister works with individuals, dyads (groups of two), subsystems (groups of three or more people), the system as a whole (the congregation, its life and work), the supersystem (denominational structures), and external systems that interface with the church (such as the community, neighboring churches, other denominations, etc.).

Second, an activity may be oriented toward either ideas or people, or a combination of both. The minister deals with concepts, seeks to understand deep truth and to interpret it clearly, forcefully, and persuasively either from the platform (inside or outside the church) or in face-to-face relationships. On the other hand, some activities require almost eclusive focus on a person and his needs. Both dimensions may be present in some activities.

Third, the extent of change that may be hoped for as the purpose of any particular role activity may be estimated. Some of the clergyman's activity is supportive in nature; it aims at maintaining the *status quo,* either in the individual's spiritual or mental health or in the integrity of the organization. Other activity is aimed at radical change, in the style and purpose of the church, in the values of the community, in the power structures of society, in the lives of persons, or in unhappy homes, etc.

Finally, we may examine a minister's style. Since this is determined in many respects by his particular personality and beliefs about working with people, it may tend to be more or less constant in different situations. However, varied styles increase his competence. At times, his effectiveness will depend upon his being authoritative and directive. At other times, he must be highly permissive and responsive to delicate nuances of feeling. He must understand group processes and effective styles of intervention to bring about change.

Let us illustrate with only one dimension—*status quo* vs. change.

Table 8   SOME VARIABLES INVOLVED IN THE PERFORMANCE OF CLERGY ROLES

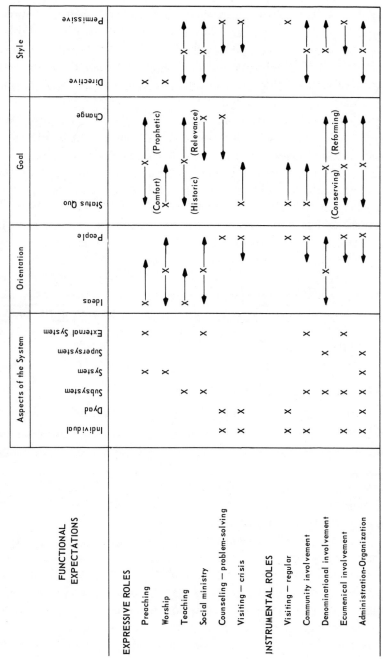

FUNCTIONAL EXPECTATIONS	Aspects of the System						Orientation		Goal		Style	
	Individual	Dyad	Subsystem	System	Supersystem	External System	Ideas	People	Status Quo	Change	Directive	Permissive
EXPRESSIVE ROLES												
Preaching				X		X	X		X (Comfort) ↕ X (Prophetic)		X	
Worship				X			X ↕	↑	X ↕		X	
Teaching			X				X ↕	X ↕	X (Historic) ↕ X (Relevance)		↕	X
Social ministry			X			X	↕	X ↕	↕	X	↕	X
Counseling – problem-solving	X	X						X		X	↕	↕
Visiting – crisis	X	X						X ↕	X		↕	X
INSTRUMENTAL ROLES												
Visiting – regular	X	X						X	X			X
Community involvement	X		X			X	X ↕	X ↕	X	↑	↕	X
Denominational involvement			X		X		↕	↕	X (Conserving) ↕ X (Reforming)		↕	X
Ecumenical involvement	X		X			X	X ↕	X ↕	↕	X	↕	X
Administration-Organization	X	X	X	X	X		X ↕	X ↕	↕	↑	↕	↕

(Refer to Table 8, column entitled "Goal.") When the minister preaches, he may be seeking to comfort and confirm in the faith, or he may speak prophetically with the purpose of stirring his people to radical action. He may be somewhere between these poles—for instance, interpreting eternal truth in such a way as to promote gradual change and growth. His teaching may emphasize historic values or relevant action, or both. His counseling may seek to be supportive or to help someone break through to new life in the solution of a problem. His involvement in the community may be that of Rotarian or of crusader. Within his presbytery, conference, or synod, he may aim to conserve the strengths of his denominational heritage or to reform the system. Needless to say, these alternative stances will be conditioned by the particular orientation a man has to his ministry, but most men will find themselves called upon to work for the *status quo* on some issues or for change on others.

Taking into account all the different dimensions suggested in our analysis, plus others that will occur to the practicing clergyman, one is forced to the conclusion that a minister's versatility in the playing of different roles is not only a virtue to be desired but a necessity for survival.

All Things to All Men—Rapid Fire

It is hardly a new insight to claim that the minister is called upon to be all things to all men. That which needs to be stressed at this point is the way in which these varied role pressures pile, one upon the other, in rapid fire. It is not that the clergyman is caught in the cross fire from several snipers with high-powered rifles. A more apt analogy may be that of machine guns, grenades, and booby traps going off around him all at once.

Again, we need to beware lest we picture the clergyman as being the only one who has to face complex role pressures. Nothing could be farther from the truth. Sarbin and Allen (123) point to the complexity of role performance as being a common phenomenon. Most individuals feel the pressure of simultaneous competitive or conflicting role obligations. They must shift from one role to another, apportion their time and energy among alternative roles, and resolve role conflicts. Furthermore, the rapid movement from one role expectation to another may add confusion to one's understanding of his roles. Unless the transition from one role to the next is clear and precise, the earlier role may tend to influence adversely performance of the later role.

Thus, as the minister moves from preaching to problem-solving counseling, he must quickly reorient himself to a completely different set of expectations if he is to be successful in performing the new role.

Figure B suggests a shorthand symbolic framework with which to

Figure B   SYMBOLIC FRAMEWORK FOR PICTURING ROLE DEMANDS

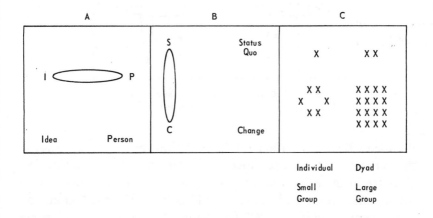

picture the role demands along several dimensions at once. The horizontal orbit indicated in box A represents the alternating movement that the minister must successfully negotiate in changing from a role that is primarily oriented toward *ideas* (represented by symbol "I") to a role that is primarily oriented toward *people* (symbol "P"). Thus, one of the clergyman's orbits revolves around either ideas or people.

The vertical orbit indicated in box B represents movement between the polarities of maintaining the *status quo* ("S") or working for *change* ("C"). In box C, we find the symbolic representation of the different sizes and compositions of groups with which the clergyman is involved. He works with individuals (the "X" in the upper left-hand corner), with dyads (the two "X's" in the upper right-hand corner), with small groups (lower left-hand corner), and with large groups or systems (lower right-hand corner).

Putting all these symbols together, we have in Figure C a representation of two role performances of a clergyman. When he teaches

Figure C   REPRESENTATION OF TWO ROLE PERFORMANCES
OF A CLERGYMAN

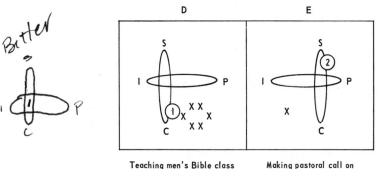

Teaching men's Bible class   Making pastoral call on
on Jeremiah   a dying parishioner

the men's Bible class (box D) he is dealing mainly with ideas, so the vertical orbit is placed toward the left, near "I" for ideas. His objective in the class is to bring about a change in attitudes toward social issues, so the ball numbered "1" is located at the bottom end of the vertical orbit near "C" for change. Under the two orbits are six "X's" in a circle, representing the small group with which the minister is working.

Similarly, when the pastor is calling upon a dying parishioner in the hospital (box E), he is working intimately with a person (the vertical orbit located at the symbol "P") and is seeking to help support that individual with the eternal verities of his faith as he faces the last realities of death. The ball for role performance 2 is, therefore, located at the zenith of its orbit near "S" for *status quo*. One "X" symbolizes the one-to-one relationship of pastor and parishioner.

Taking this symbolic shorthand as a method of representing the varied role pressures exerted upon the minister during the course of a day, we might look at Figure D and trace these activities in orbit from role performance 1, inside the large circle (center left) clock-

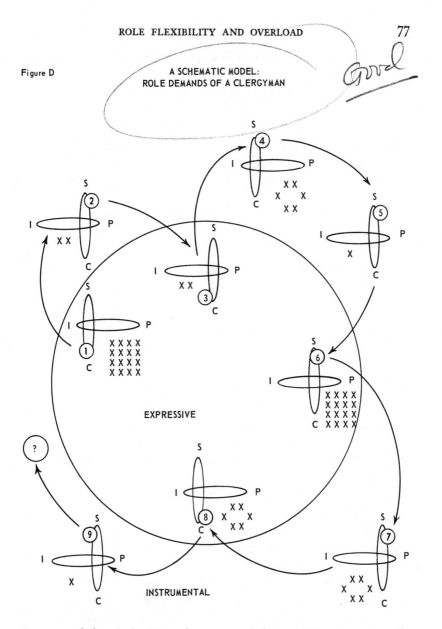

Figure D

A SCHEMATIC MODEL:
ROLE DEMANDS OF A CLERGYMAN

EXPRESSIVE

INSTRUMENTAL

wise around the circle. Note that some of the activities are primarily *expressive* of the basic purposes of the church and are thus located *inside* the large circle, which is "expressive" territory. Role acts 1, 3, 6, and 8 are thus seen to be expressive acts. Other acts (2, 4, 5, 7, and 9) are fundamentally *instrumental* to the maintenance and growth of the organization and are therefore represented as being *outside* the large circle in "instrumental" territory. We trace the different tasks of the minister through the day as follows:

1. He preaches a *prophetic* sermon: an expressive act, idea-oriented, directed toward change, involving a large group.

2. He visits a new resident in the community, welcoming him and inviting him to participate in the life of the church: an instrumental act, person-oriented, directed toward the *status quo* (i.e., maintaining the membership of the church), involving a dyad (husband and wife).

3. He counsels with a couple who are on the verge of divorce: an expressive act, person-oriented, directed toward change (in the unhealthy marriage relationship), involving another dyad.

4. He meets with church officers to plan the every member canvass: an instrumental act, idea-oriented (how to conduct the canvass), directed toward the *status quo* (maintaining the income of the church), involving a small group. NOTE: Some might argue, with reason, that this could be an expressive activity (since stewardship is an outpouring of basic Christian commitment) or that the activity is directed toward change (since it is desired that people increase their giving in response to the canvass).

5. He calls a member on the telephone to persuade him to accept responsibility as a church school teacher: an instrumental act (to secure a needed teacher), person-oriented, directed toward the *status quo* (maintaining the church school), involving a single person.

6. He conducts a funeral: an instrumental act, oriented to both ideas and people, directed toward the *status quo* (comfort via eternal verities), involving a large group.

7. He attends a meeting of Rotary officers: an instrumental act (maintaining relationships with community leaders), oriented toward people (the interest in relationships is his primary reason for being there), directed toward the *status quo,* involving a small group of people.

8. He has an evening meeting with his session on fair housing: an expressive act, oriented toward ideas, directed toward change, involving a small group.

9. He has a late-night consultation with one of his elders to attempt resolution of a personality clash: an instrumental act, person-oriented, directed toward the *status quo* (preserving a relationship), involving a single person.

Readers who examine this carefully may not agree with the way in which any particular role act has been classified. This may well reflect their particular styles or values or goals of ministry. Some will recognize that certain dimensions of the ministerial task have been left out of this picture altogether. For example, not only does the minister work with *ideas* and with *people*. He also must deal with *things* such as church buildings, hymnbooks, or perhaps even mimeograph machines. However, the point has already been made, and we shall not make this analysis more complicated than necessary. Many different styles, goals, and relations are involved in the activities of a minister, and these come in rapid succession. To use another figure of speech, the minister must shift gears quickly and smoothly if he is to be effective. What Fichter has shown for the urban parish seems to apply to the work of every minister: "The present dynamic situation in the urban American parish seems to require not so much the emphasis on one role more than another, as a simultaneous coordination of multiple roles." (97:86.)

Many Tasks Make Heavy Work

One final word must be said regarding role overload. The hypothetical illustrations just given not only demonstrate the demand for role flexibility but give some feeling for the heavy load of expectations to which the clergyman must respond. Most ministers work very long hours at highly demanding tasks. The Episcopal study finds an average workweek for parish priests of 66.7 hours. While there may be other professions that average longer hours, few require the range of responses demanded of the minister.

Again, the clergyman is not alone in feeling that he cannot meet the sheer volume of expectations that others have of him. Among male wage and salary workers 45 percent indicate they are disturbed because they feel they have such a heavy workload that "they cannot possibly finish during an ordinary work day," while 43 percent feel that the amount of work expected of them interferes with the quality of their performance. (76:59.)

What we are suggesting is that "role overload" may be perceived as role conflict. Even though all the sent expectations from the minister's role set are legitimate and are logically compatible with one another, the minister will feel conflicted if within the available time he cannot possibly complete all the tasks urged upon him by others (and by his own conscience). He must then set priorities, deciding which pressures he can meet and which he may postpone. If all pressures are equally insistent and cannot be denied, the conflict may become intolerable. (77.)

The reader, who has persisted patiently through analysis after analysis, will have cried out long ago, "What in the world can the minister do about all this?" The remaining chapters will address themselves to this question.

PART
II
WHAT TO DO ABOUT ROLE
AMBIGUITY AND CONFLICT

What can the minister do about role ambiguity and role conflict? What should he do? To what extent is it even desirable to clarify expectations and resolve differences, if that is possible?

The easy first answer to these questions is not necessarily the right answer. To begin with, as Blizzard has pointed out, "the ministry is a free profession with diffuse role definitions in a voluntary institution. Diversity of role performance and lack of clarity is to be expected." (19:15.) Furthermore, it seems that many of the clergy are attracted to the ministry by the challenge of diversity. Some role conflict may make the work more interesting to them, since they are exhilarated by the demand for versatility and by the opportunity to use problem-solving skills, and since theirs is a total commitment which has always been characteristic of the profession. To seek narrowly defined and rigid job definitions for the minister not only might limit his creativity and professional autonomy but also might undercut the motivation of the best members of the profession. "Rigidly to structure the role and functions of the ministry is to ossify them and, consequently, to render them relatively functionless in relation to society." (60.) Ashbrook's research, which will be elaborated later, suggests that the minister who is most effective in the opinion of his congregation and in his own eyes, seems to have "(a) enough satisfaction with each of the tasks necessary to meet the varying demands of the local church (both expressive and instrumental), yet (b) enough dissatisfaction to keep the minister sensitive to his people and the realities of his situation" (12:24).

In favor of continued role conflict, under certain circumstances, is the probability that a change in norms and expectations may be very necessary for the good of society and for the health of the church. Such change must necessarily involve conflict. Key people in the change process may be called to live at the tension points of conflict. In fact, as a prophet of the Lord, the minister may be called to exactly such conflict.

While one might argue that the tranquillity of social groups is to be preferred to abrasiveness within such groups, there is a strong prophetic tradition which would suggest that the opposite goal might better be pursued by the clergy if religion is to have any meaning in a time of rapid social change. . . . The goal . . . could just as well be toward exposing the raw nerves of dissent, hidden agendas and diverse perspectives, rather than searching for consensus or the reduction (or avoidance) of group tension. (50:26.)

There is a tendency in the church to resolve conflicts too quickly in the name of "reconciliation," perhaps because some are unwilling to bear the pain of creative conflict. Comfortable, quick solutions to conflicts are often not the best solutions. Effective leaders must be willing to pay the price of creative conflict. They must "live at the precise points of conflict between old norms and new aspirations, in the open place between the disintegrated cultural model of the past and the as yet undesigned styles of life for the future" (79:51).

So there is a definite place for conflict and ambiguity in church life. Nevertheless it is clear that role conflict and ambiguity are often unnecessary and undesirable, as well as very costly in human resources. The energy spent in trying to deal with ambiguity (that might have been avoided) could be spent in creative and productive activity. The time spent in fulfilling misunderstood "expectations," or in accomplishing tasks that could much better be handled by someone other than the minister, is a terrible waste of the church's manpower. The lack of definition of the minister's task, which causes misunderstandings that might have been avoided, compounds anxieties and leads to heartbreak and misery, is really inexcusable in an age when relatively effective methods have been developed for dealing with such matters.

Furthermore, there seem to be limits to the degree of either ambiguity or role conflict that different personalities can tolerate. As Kahn and his colleagues (76) have discovered, introverts have more difficulty in enduring the stress of social pressure; those who are emotionally sensitive experience greater internal tension under a given degree of external conflict, and those who are strongly achievement-oriented and deeply involved in their work may experience more role conflict than those who are not so involved. Interestingly, those who are relatively flexible are subjected to stronger social pressures than those who have already demonstrated by their rigidity the futility of applying such pressures. Extreme or persistent conflict and ambiguity can be damaging to the individual since they cannot be meaningfully integrated into a person's existing self-concept and are thus identity-destroying. (76:6.)

What is needed, then, is a much more self-conscious understanding by the minister of these questions so that he can exercise more control over the conflicts and ambiguities that relate to his calling. If he has chosen to maintain or accept as inevitable certain areas of ambiguity or role conflict for the sake of his professional calling and in the service of the mission of the church, that is one thing. If he makes such choices, knowing the cost involved, that is quite a different situation from finding himself trapped in ambiguities and conflicts that he was not able to anticipate and is unable to ameliorate. It is the latter condition to which we should now address ourselves.

Before we move to a more careful examination of alternative courses of action for the minimizing and management of role conflict and ambiguity, it is well to make clear, as perhaps the analysis up to this point has already succeeded in doing, that there are available no ready-made or easy solutions. We are dealing with a deeply rooted religious heritage and a complex set of interrelationships; with values, personalities, experiences, expectations, etc., that interact within structures and systems of considerable complexity. There is a great deal of difference from one situation to another in the role demands made upon the minister. To assume, therefore, that there is some "ideal role model" for the clergyman, which can be discovered, which can be understood, interpreted, taught, or imposed, is to misunderstand completely the dynamics of society, of systems within it, and of change. As James Anderson observes, we must dispose of the myth that the solution can be found in the statement, "Let's get the role straight, inculcate it in the clergy, and see that the laity understand it." (9:9–10.)

Accordingly, we will not be looking at some kind of ideal role model, nor at solutions to role conflict problems that will be applicable to all situations. Instead, we will be suggesting different processes or methods of approach which the minister can apply as they may fit his situation. There are a number of issues that must be dealt with through a total systems approach. These will be elaborated in Chapter 7. However, we shall begin with suggestions directed primarily to the minister himself, since he is the prime actor in his own role set.

CHAPTER 6

Minimize and Reduce Ambiguity

It is perhaps obvious that a fundamental approach to role conflict and ambiguity is to prevent it from taking place, or (since that is not completely possible) to minimize it. Any process that will ensure a thorough discussion and clarification of role expectations before the minister undertakes a new work will presumably serve as valuable insurance against unanticipated role pressures. In considering a call, both the minister and the pulpit nominating committee should give very careful consideration to such questions as: What is the meaning and purpose of the church? What is the mission of this particular congregation? What do people of this congregation expect in a minister? Are those expectations relevant to their goals? Does the minister share the understandings and goals of the congregation? Do their expectations fit reasonably well with his expectations, with his professional concerns, personal needs, predispositions and style of ministry? Presumably most ministers and committees deal with many of these questions in some way. The difficulty comes in that they may not have faced them systematically, explicitly, and at sufficient depth to make certain they have uncovered any potential booby traps in the proposed relationship before it is entered into. Any help that the church-at-large can give to both clergy and pulpit committee to ensure a thorough process of clarifying role expectations and of matching role expectations with potential role performance should go far in minimizing ambiguity and unnecessary conflict. Ultimately, however, it is the minister himself who must make certain that every possible expectation of any importance has been put on the table and looked at carefully.

Know Yourself

If one is to minimize ambiguity in the expectations of others, he must also minimize it in himself. Confusion breeds confusion. Clarity of purpose will help others to define their purposes too. The person who is not clear as to who he is, what he believes, what his understanding of the church and the ministry is, what his goals are, and where his strengths and weaknesses lie, is not well prepared to evaluate or relate to the expectations of others for his performance in any particular parish. (24.) In considering a call, the man is better prepared who can say: "This is who I am. Here is what I do well. Here is what you cannot really expect of me, but must be arranged for in some other way." Such a man is less likely to experience unanticipated role conflict and is more likely to discover a place of service where he can make a maximum contribution.

Know yourself. What roles do you really enjoy playing? What is your role repertoire? How flexible are you in fulfilling different types of role expectations? What is your tolerance for ambiguity and for conflict?

If, as is commonly recognized, there is widespread uncertainty regarding the Christian faith and the purpose of the church, it is incumbent upon the minister to do everything in his power to be clear in his own mind and heart on these questions. This of course does not imply that a minister should use clarity as an excuse for dogmatism but rather that through dialogue with different perspectives he will find continual opportunity to be growing in his understanding of his calling. Thus role pressure may become the occasion for a clearer elaboration of who he is, what he stands for, and what he is called to be and to do.

An Actor More than a Reactor

Ashbrook comments on these concerns by emphasizing the importance of the minister's becoming a "responding-responsible person." "That means cultivating a heightened sense of I-ness, so that the clergyman experiences himself as subject more than object, as actor more than re-actor. He must respond from a center of inwardness and stop manipulating or being manipulated by himself and others. As actor, he is a molder of events more than a prisoner of events. . . . Just as Jesus brought content to his role as Messiah," so "the clergyman . . . can color the content of his role by bringing his own expectations to bear upon those of the laity. In such a transactional process lies the dynamic of and for change." (11:35–36.)

Thus, to return to the negotiation of a psychological contract in a new pastorate, the minister must take the initiative in making clear who he is and what he can be expected to do. He is in a strong position if he is able to say, "As a professional, you can rely on me to meet your expectations in *these* areas, but *those* expectations really are not within my professional competence." Such self-knowledge, as Thomas Brown, director of the Northeast Career Center, has pointed out, is one of the important contributions that career counseling can make to the clergyman.

Career counseling may also help the clergyman distinguish between who he is as a person and the roles he plays as a minister. As we have seen, this is a point of particular stress for him.

Check Your Perceptions

As has been suggested in the initial discussion of role ambiguity, many a seeming conflict in clergy roles may in reality be an evidence of ambiguity rather than of conflict per se. Or at least, when the ambiguity has been reduced, the conflict that remains may be more tolerable. Hence, in a role stress situation, it is important to begin by trying to reduce ambiguity.

Since the *perceived* role expectation is often not the same as the *sent* role expectation, it is important to allow for the possibility that the conflict one *feels* in the expectations is not matched by *real* expectations. In other words, to use Kahn's terms, the "psychological environment" of a person may not correspond to his "objective environment."

The results of several studies suggest that, for whatever reasons, clergymen do not accurately assess the feelings of their people about their work. Ashbrook, for example, found that a person who was most satisfied with being a minister "tended to be most impressed with the results of his ministry." Neither his feelings of satisfaction nor his perception of his effectiveness seemed to have much relationship to the way church members assessed "his effectiveness, the success of the church, or the adequacy of its religious training."

The man who was dissatisfied with being a minister, with the expressive tasks of leading worship and preaching, and with the instrumental task of cooperating with other churches was rated by his members as doing an effective job. (12:21–22.)

Ashbrook suggests that this discrepancy may arise because the minister who experiences fulfillment in his work tends to see the impressive results he wants to see. Conversely, one might suppose that dissatisfaction makes one feel less effective. In other words, the minister, in a very human way, tends to measure his work by his own feelings about it, rather than by any objective criteria.

Falk finds that "generally the ministers tend to underestimate . . . the amount of disagreement between themselves and their parishioners" (44). Didier, on the other hand, concludes that pastors feel *more* role conflict than seems actually to be present. He finds that their perceptions of the expectations of their people differ considerably from the actual expectations. Consistently, they tend to believe that significant others are more conservative, demanding, and restrictive than is actually the case. He concludes that pastors tend to respond "in ways that indicate a desire for more autonomy and self-direction than they perceive that significant others would allow." (35.)

Mills suggests that one reason ministers distrust the positive feedback they get from their congregations is that compliments are too readily forthcoming, no matter how insignificant their accomplishments. Pastors have discovered that this easy praise is not necessarily related to the leadership they have exercised. "Hence a distinction is necessary between *visible* feedback which is a reliable indicator of success and that which is merely verbal." (101:104.)

Maier describes a denomination-wide program in 1962 in which 10,000 United Presbyterians participated in 144 three-day seminars on The Nature of the Ministry. Separate seminars were held for ministers and laymen. Ministers, in general, were disturbed by discussions involving their status. Laymen, on the other hand, were excited by the opportunity to discuss such fundamental questions. He concludes:

One striking revelation of these seminars was the fact that there is so little real communication between ministers and laymen. By and large, they are not hearing one another. Laymen have heard the gospel verbally, but seldom in any way that is really meaningful to them. What *they think* the minister is saying is not what *he* thinks he is saying—and that is not simply a matter of vocabulary. The ministers, in turn, frequently do not know what the laymen are thinking and feeling deep inside, or what their real questions are. (The laymen are, for the most part, too polite to ask them.)

In a few seminars held as follow-up to the original round, some ministers and laymen have been brought together for discussions of the ministry we all share. Where this has occurred, there is almost always a shocked recognition, particularly on the part of the laymen, that even here communication is not taking place on a meaningful level. Where the confrontation can continue long enough (several days is usually needed), there is usually a breakthrough of some proportions, accompanied by gratitude on the part of both groups. Such groups have said very earnestly that the dialogue between ministry and laity *must continue.* Here, in fact, is the best hope for the renewal of the church in our time, because only as the dialogue is continued in depth is there a likelihood of meaningful joint activity as both groups seek to witness in a rapidly moving world. (93:28.)

Establish and Maintain Communication

If the foregoing says anything at all, it cries out for better communication between the minister and his role set. The best hope for reduction of role conflict and ambiguity is in the opening of "honest communication between the clergy with their theological expectation of people and the people with their 'organizational expectations' of clergymen" (130:10).

Leiffer's recent study (88) found that most ministers (between 76.7 percent and 81.9 percent) believed that the essential functions of a pastor are considerably *different* today than a generation ago. Similar percentages of the same ministers (69.4 percent to 81.8 percent), however, felt that the layman assumes his functions are the *same* as a generation ago. More than half (50.1 percent to 59.4 percent) of the pastors believed that the conventional conceptions of the minister held by lay people "prevented them from leading a normal life and being themselves."

Whether or not these perceptions are accurate, the discrepancy in the minds of the clergy provides a rather eloquent argument for the importance of establishing better communication between clergy and laity. Through better communication, either the ministers might discover they were wrong in their feelings about the laity, or the laity might achieve a more realistic understanding of the demands involved in the task of the clergy. At least, there would be likelihood of their moving more closely together in their understanding of the ministry.

The Episcopal study (43, Report 9:19) provides evidence that further reinforces the need for communication. When members of the vestry were asked for the most difficult problem they had with clergymen, the highest percentage of response (19 percent) was "lack of communication or understanding." Seventeen percent said "budget" and 9 percent said "failure to define roles, responsibilities, goals, techniques, etc." Over one fourth (28 percent) of the causes of conflict between priests and vestry seem to be related directly to poor communication. How many other conflicts were really caused by poor communication, without being identified as such, is impossible to say. One cannot help feeling, for example, that even problems in the area of budget might be ameliorated if a process of careful planning were instituted that involved the setting of goals and the conducting of periodic reviews. Thus, perhaps 45 percent of the conflicts identified by the vestry might be helped by effective patterns of communication, planning, and review. These, of course, are rather fundamental to the functioning of an effective organization.

Of course, automatic benefits do not accrue following the inauguration of planning and review techniques. A great deal depends upon how they are conceived and carried out. For example, when performance review takes place at budget-making time or in connection with salary review, each process may interfere with the proper exercise of the other. Performance review is more likely to be unbiased if it takes place at a completely different time from budget decisions. Church officers do not then have to consider the minister's effectiveness in threatening proximity to a decision on the salary increase he wants, with the corresponding threat to their balanced budget.

Don't Run Away

Increased communication is especially important when the minister is experiencing role conflict or ambiguity. Yet research suggests that at such times communication is likely to *decrease* rather than to increase. Kahn and his associates (76) have discovered that those who experience a great deal of role conflict tend to discount the importance and power of role senders, to trust them less, like them less personally, and withdraw from contacts with them. Similar, although less severe reactions are evident under conditions of ambiguity, especially when the focal person is uncertain how his associates evaluate him or whether or not they are satisfied with his behavior. Under such circumstances it is more difficult to trust, respect, or like them.

Falk found that when parishioners disagree among themselves in their expectations, "ministers tend to repudiate unacceptable expectations or redefine their roles. However, when parishioners consensually disagree with their minister, he tends to become depressed rather than to react in an overt fashion." (44.) In other words, under concerted role conflict, ministers tend to withdraw psychologically.

Withdrawal is a self-defeating mechanism. Whereas it is aimed at reducing role conflict, it actually initiates a vicious cycle that *increases* conflict. When one withdraws, he cuts off communication and greatly reduces the flow of information between the role receiver and his senders. This, in turn, makes available less data with which anyone can work to resolve the conflict. Cooperation and negotiation become impossible. In frustration, the role senders increase their pressure on the focal person and "invoke stronger sanctions" in an effort to make him "hear" and respond favorably (76:70).

The tendency toward withdrawal may be even more pronounced when role ambiguity arises out of a doubt about the way in which one's role senders are evaluating the focal person's performance. To seek clarification of the appraisal of others is to run the risk of discovering that one's worst fears are well founded. "For some people it is easier to fear the worst than to know the worst about oneself." (76:91.) A safe course of action then may be to retreat into uncertainty in order to protect one's self-esteem. In fact, there is evidence that "unfavorable and often uncommunicated evaluations by associates are experienced by the focal person as ambiguity about how he is evaluated. . . . The more the associates of a focal person see him as emotionally unstable, as lacking assertive self-confidence, as being unbusinesslike or unsociable, the more uncertain he is about how satisfied they are with him." (76:93.)

How, then, is the minister to deal with the question of feedback? If he is afraid of it, his need for it may be even greater than if he welcomes it. In that case, he may do well to consider securing the help of a competent psychological counselor to enable him to accept himself more fully and thus be more open to a continual process of meaningful communication with the key members of his role set. As Kahn has pointed out, "a meaningful self-identity rests in part on clear and consistent feedback from those around us" (76:93). Therefore, in the face of a conflict, when one is tempted to withdraw, he will do well to remind himself that a more effective course of action is to increase the amount of communication with his role set, and to engage them as information gatherers and providers. "Many people in organizations use just this method. If they are unclear about what they can do at some time or about what others expect of them, they go and ask; they seek clarity by means of increased communications." (76:91.)

Discussion Reduces Role Conflict

Research conducted by Higgins and Dittes in the church councils of two congregations has produced highly suggestive and helpful evidence that discussion of the minister's role by clergy and laity facilitates increased consensus among laymen concerning the role expectations of the minister, and increased agreement between the minister and laymen. In one of the churches, discussion centered around what priority the minister should give to different possible activities. In the other, discussion concerned the method or style of his leadership. In each church an attitude survey was taken before and after the discussion.

Each church found a significant increase in the amount of agreement between pastor and people, but *only* on the subjects discussed by that church, and *not* on the subjects discussed by the other church.

Thus, each church council served as a control group on the other. In general, it was found that the more discussion there was of any given role subject, the more agreement developed. There was one important exception to this finding. Increase toward consensus was not demonstrated on the topic of administrative and organizational responsibilities. Apparently, this was the case because there was so much agreement between laymen and minister on this subject at the outset that "there was little room for improvement." The largest changes in laymen's attitudes came in their understanding of the importance of study to the minister; a reduced emphasis on routine parish calling; and increased importance given to the training of lay leadership.

One significant qualification needs to be kept in mind in applying these findings. Those who participate in the role discussions must have a high level of commitment to the church or institution involved. This was a basic theoretical assumption on which the experiments were designed, and those selected to participate were judged to have such commitment. In this case, the commitment of each layman was measured by the amount of his annual contribution to the church. A correlation was found between this index of "church commitment" and increase in agreement with the minister. This rather startling evidence of change among those who might be expected to throw their weight around on behalf of the *status quo* undoubtedly needs further study. Nevertheless, these research findings have rather far-reaching implications for the resolution of role conflict. As Higgins and Dittes suggest, in addition to research possibilities, the questionnaires they developed might well be used by churches for a program of self-study, "both for stimulating discussion and also for assessing its effects." They also point to a number of questions that should be kept in mind in applying the methods of this study to other situations in the parish.

The discussions in this study were led, not by a member of the council or by the minister, but by a stranger. Was it possibly his "neutrality" between minister and layman which was the most important factor in producing the noted effects? Was it the fact that minister and layman were reduced, as rarely happens in local church meetings, to more or less equal status as fellow discussants?

The discussion leader took the role of a fairly passive clarifier of issues as discussants themselves posed them. What if he had more aggressively stated and defined the issues at the outset, or probed individual persons' attitudes and background motivations?

The discussion was entered into "cold," with the topic chosen by the experimenter, not by the minister or the laymen. . . . What if the discussion had been precipitated by a particular instance of role conflict in the church, or at least had been introduced by asking participants to recall particular incidents? (71:22.)

Another fairly dramatic evidence of the value of discussing one's role conflicts comes from Project Laity, conducted by the former Department of the Church and Economic Life of the National Council of Churches. Experimental adult education programs were developed in twenty-eight churches in three different cities. Ministers were asked to serve as resource members of the groups, rather than in their usual authority-oriented roles as designated leaders. Their function was to enable the group to "determine its own learning goals, help in its problem-solving and planning efforts, and . . . maintain effective intragroup relationships." (13:28–29.)

This change in the usual role expectations resulted in role conflicts, with which clergymen dealt in different ways. Some openly shared with their groups the role conflicts they felt. These groups helped to resolve the conflicts and continued to function to the end of the project. Others attempted to cover up the role conflicts they were experiencing. Without exception, these groups terminated their activity before the end of the project. In other words, the longevity of a group's life was closely related to the readiness of its minister-resource-member to share his role conflicts and work them through with his group.

CHAPTER 7

Manage Your Conflict

It is clear from everything that has been said up to this point that no one can expect to find himself in a situation without role conflict. A number of steps have been suggested by which the minister can clarify ambiguity and keep conflict to a minimum. But conflict there will be. The important question is, How is it dealt with? If, after resisting the temptation to withdraw, the clergyman has sought to clarify his roles with members of his role set but still faces role conflict, what then?

Study the Dynamics of Your Role Set

To begin with, it will be helpful to examine the role set carefully in order to determine the nature of the role conflicts that exist and the variety and strength of the forces that are operating. In particular, the interrelationships among four dimensions may provide helpful clues as to alternative courses of action (99).

1. *How deeply involved in the role relationships are the different role senders?* For some of them, the relationship may be of peripheral concern. To others it may be of central importance. A failure to fulfill an expectation will be of much less consequence to the former than it will be to the latter. A member of the board of trustees who opposes the pastor and the church officers may be so involved in his business that his conflict with the minister may assume minor importance. He may not feel it worth his while

to press his case. On the other hand, business reversals may make him press for "success" in the church.

2. *How powerful is each member of the role set?* What sanctions can one or another apply? What penalties or rewards may be expected from them? What coalitions of power exist? Are groups more powerful than single role senders who might otherwise have a decisive voice? In weighing the power of a role sender, one should take into account the extent of his involvement (discovered in item 1, above). As the foregoing illustration has suggested, a powerful role sender who has only a casual investment in the relationship may not choose to exercise his power, or may be so involved in other concerns that the conflict in which you are involved may be of little consequence to him.

3. *How observable to members of the role set are the role conflicts?* As has already been suggested, the ministry as a whole is at a decided disadvantage in comparison with other professions in that most of the role activities of the clergyman are highly visible. Not all of them are visible, however, nor must all remain as visible as they are. For example, the growing trend for ministers to own their manses and to buy them at some distance from the church is a step in the direction of reducing visibility and of separating the minister's professional life from his personal life.

4. *How legitimate are the different claims being made on the minister by those involved in the conflict?* It would appear on the surface that a minister might give the most weight to role expectations that have the greatest legitimacy. This is not a foregone conclusion, however. A study of school superintendents suggests that there are actually three interrelated factors, or dimensions, that must be considered: (*a*) the legitimacy of the expectations; (*b*) the sanctions, or penalties, that may be applied if the expectations are ignored; and (*c*) the tendency of the focal person to give priority either to legitimacy or to sanctions.

Gross and others analyzed the solutions to intra-role conflict adopted by superintendents of schools. (59.) They found that, in any given conflict situation between alternative expectations A and B, there are four possible behaviors to achieve conflict resolution: (1) to conform to expectation A; (2) to conform to expectation B;

(3) to perform some compromise behavior (that conforms in part to both); and (4) to avoid conforming to either A or B. They demonstrated that most of the choices made could be predicted if they had knowledge about the three factors mentioned above.

First, they needed to know *how superintendents felt about the legitimacy or illegitimacy of each incompatible expectation.* If legitimacy were the only dimension, the choice would favor the expectation perceived to be legitimate. Second, they needed to know *how superintendents perceived the sanctions that might be applied* if they chose one or the other alternative. What penalties might be brought to bear upon them in either event? Again, if this were the only dimension, prediction would favor an alternative involving lesser penalty or greater reward. Of course, in actual situations both legitimacy and sanctions were involved. When an alternative was seen to have greater legitimacy and less stringent sanctions, the choice for that alternative could be predicted. However, when the alternative was seen to be of great legitimacy coupled with painful sanctions, more information was needed in order to predict the decision. The third factor in Gross's analysis was the *disposition or tendency of the superintendent to give priority to legitimacy over sanctions* (called a "moral orientation") *or to give primacy to sanctions over legitimacy* (called an "expedient orientation"). Still another disposition found in some superintendents was to give equal weight to sanctions and legitimacy. These were called moral-expedients.

Using this theoretical framework, Gross found that decisions between incompatible expectations could be predicted 96 percent correctly for the "expedients," 92 percent correctly for the "moral-expedients," and 82 percent correctly for the "moralists."

Focus Your Roles

If one is seeking to reduce role conflict, it may prove fruitful to consider the possibility of changing the role expectations with which one is dealing. Sarbin and Allen suggest that it is sometimes possible to merge conflicting roles into a single new compromise role that eliminates the conflict. Dittes (36) proposes that the minister use such an approach in resolving the conflict between his administrative-organizational responsibilities and his pastoral activities.

The most common proposed solution, he says, is for the minister to make a clear-cut choice between one or the other. He then is free to approach all his tasks from the administrative stance or to slough off all administration and engage in some form of "pure ministry." Dittes' solution, however, accepts both instrumental and expressive tasks, and seeks to *integrate* them through a recognition that administrative responsibilities often provide occasions when one sees people as they really are, with their true selves revealed and their real problems exposed. Thus administrative and organizational tasks become opportunities for "vital encounters and valid occasions for creative ministry." As he makes clear, "It is in the administrative snarls that one is far more likely to find passions aroused, masks lowered, neat roles abandoned, stubborn resistances revealed, and glimmering aspirations bared" (36:118). Then one can be at the heart of the expressive task of ministering to these conditions. Reuel Howe finds similar possibilities for ministry when clergy "accept the inevitable tensions between the church as an institution and the church as mission and look for its creative possibilities" (72:218). Evidence of this can be found in Ashbrook's research (12), which showed that

> no minister who was satisfied with administration received a low rating by members on effectiveness, adequacy of religious training, and church success, nor did he rate the results of his own ministry as low; in some instances he received high ratings on these effects.

Ashbrook found that the effective and successful pastor was the "man whose leadership was instrumentally skillful and inspiring—who could define roles, structure expectations, and take initiative—and whose leadership at the same time was expressively tolerant of uncertainty in the group and encouraging of member freedom" (12:24). Integration of the expressive-instrumental conflict into a style of leader behavior that somehow combines both not only reduces the conflict between the two but seems to produce a creative alternative. Ashbrook finds that the successful generalist in smaller churches combines, "in a more closely integrated manner, an expressive awareness of people and an instrumental skillfulness in getting jobs done. . . . That kind of leader could handle complex problems and chaotic demands. He was skillful and inspiring. He was considerate of persons, able to sense what was going on in the

[margin handwritten note: Admin as focus for pastoral concern]

group, and could keep the group working as a unit." (12:25.) Commenting on this, Glasse (55:35) likens this description of the generalist to H. Richard Niebuhr's "pastoral director," calling it "the emerging new conception of the ministry."

Integrate Your Ministry

Applying this more widely to alternatives suggested by other authors, one may conclude that an effective resolution of clergy role conflict may be achieved through the selection of some integrating total orientation to the ministry that will set the various parts of it into focus and give some basis for the setting of priorities. This is frequently a missing ingredient in the clergyman's approach to his work. (60:187.)

Blizzard uses two helpful integrative concepts. A *master role* is the minister's own "concept of the ministry as an occupation distinguishable from the occupational role of other persons" (18:1-7). Descriptions of the master role by ministers participating in his study expressed an *ideological or theological* focus over half the time. Thirty-three percent referred to themselves in some way as "mediators between God and man"; 22 percent spoke of being a "servant of God." Over half the ministers used a *functional* dimension in their self-description: 32 percent spoke of the minister as a "servant" to others, and 21 percent called him "an example" for his people. To the extent that these concepts were consistent with the way in which those ministers actually integrated and organized their different roles, such thinking might help to minimize role conflict.

A minister's *integrative role* is his "goal orientation, or frame of reference to his work. . . . It is the end toward which he is working in his professional relationship with parishioners, church associations, community groups, and the general public. It is what he is trying to accomplish with people in the professional practice of religion."

Table 9 summarizes the integrating roles described by Blizzard and indicates the relative incidence of each of them in the thinking of the group of ministers he studied. The minister who seeks to bring his ministry into focus may find it helpful to think through these different integrating concepts, seeking that one of them which

Table 9

THE MINISTER'S INTEGRATING ROLES
(Based on Samuel Blizzard, 18)

	INTEGRATING ROLE TITLE	RATIO	DESCRIPTIVE SUMMARY OR ANALOGY	
	General Practitioner	1:14	Holds three or more integrating goals (balanced and same relative intensity)	
TRADITIONAL	Believer-Saint	1:14	Exemplar; man of faith; prayerfulness, submissiveness, permissiveness	IDEOLOGICAL 1:5
	Evangelist	1:12	Compelled by call to preach the Word and save souls; unshakable faith	
	Scholar	1:75	Search for truth, scholarly life, either technical religion or general	
	Liturgist	1:100	Aesthetic, liturgy as end in itself, or as means of mediating God's grace	
	Father-Shepherd	1:5	Strong man of faith; comforting father; in him, God is near; pastoral calling, serving diffuse flock	
CONTEMPORARY	Interpersonal relations specialist	1:6	Understanding and counseling; identifies with lay psychiatrists' specific work with specific persons	WORLD OF PEOPLE 2:3
	Parish promoter	1:7	Organization, smooth; objective measures; identification with businessman	
	Community problem-solver	1:10	Organizer in the community; national and international issues; prophetic; social problems	
	Educator	1:25	Communicate faith by education at each age level appropriately and comprehensively	OTHER 1:5
	Subcultural specialist	1:50	Perspective of group to which he ministers; rural, urban, ethnic, suburban	
	"Lay" minister	1:25	Implicit anticlericalism; lay identification; priesthood of all believers	
	Representative of the church-at-large	1:50	Christlike Rotarian; no parish limits; "friend of man"; ministers to all	
	Church politician	1:100	Organization man; system conformity; stress connectional or cooperative work	

comes closest to his primary values. After doing this, and with the stimulus of this framework, he may then wish to try writing down, for his own benefit, the major objectives of his ministry.

As one reads through the literature, he will discover a number of other approaches to focusing one's ministry. Luke Smith studied 22 clergymen to discover their feelings of conflict about the way they spent their time. He defined conflict operationally as irritation over time consumed by one role at the expense of another. Nine of his subjects saw themselves as *counselors*. Thirteen had a primary orientation *other than counseling*. He found that "the least strain occurred when counseling was openly acknowledged as the central role" (129). There was comparatively little conflict among those who focused on ritual, but much greater conflict among those who saw preaching as their major function. In interpreting results such as this, one must remember that the sample involved was exceedingly small, and the findings of such a study can be little more than suggestive.

Plyler's study of 63 Methodist ministers in Missouri finds a difference in the role orientation of ministers in churches of over six hundred members and in smaller churches. Ministers in the larger churches were more committed to a "coordinating" rather than an "originating" stance. Metropolitan and urban ministers stressed personal counseling, whereas rural ministers seem to be meeting the same type of need through a focus on preaching to personal problems.

Preaching, pastoral and priestly purposes dominated the expressed orientation of the respondents. The local situation seemed to determine, largely, which of the three would be considered most basic. However, the most excellent measure of satisfacory performance recognized by almost all the respondents was the ability "to select and inspire effective lay leadership." This implies that perhaps the basic purpose of the ministry seen here is to encourage and inspire laymen in the work of the church. (110.)

A note of realism should be struck at this point, lest the impression be given that focusing one's ministry is simply a matter of selecting one role and excluding others. The following counsel, for example, certainly suggests a focus for the ministry. However, if taken literally, it might prove devastating in most congregations, simply because they would not be prepared to accept this definition of ministry as adequately meeting their expectations. Gerald Kennedy writes:

One of the best statements expressing this necessary but lost attitude for the minister is from Dr. Floyd Doud Shafer (*Christianity Today,* Mar. 27, 1962). He writes: "Fling him into his office, tear the OFFICE sign from the door and nail on the sign, STUDY. Take him off the mailing list, lock him up with his books—and get him all kinds of books—and his typewriter and his Bible. . . . Force him to be the one man in our surfeited communities who knows about God. . . . Set a time clock on him that would imprison him with thought and writing about God for forty hours a week. Shut his garrulous mouth spouting remarks and stop his tongue always tripping lightly over everything non-essential. Bend his knees to the lonesome valley, and fire him from the PTA and cancel his country club membership. Rip out his telephone, burn his ecclesiastical success sheets, refuse his glad hand, put water in the gas tank of his community buggy and compel him to be a minister of the word." To which I would only comment that if this is exaggeration, it is exaggeration in the right direction. (80:95.)

Whatever else one is tempted to say about a strong statement like the foregoing, at least it leaves no doubt in the minister's mind regarding the necessity of establishing priorities and provides one possible basis for sorting out conflicting role expectations and making clear-cut decisions on the shape of one's ministry.

The Changing Person, Center Stage

Ronald Lee suggests another approach, which focuses less upon the *activities* which a minister carries out and more upon the impact of ministry upon the lives of *people*. Decisions regarding roles and functions are made in that light.

The rapid change that characterizes our age creates special needs in the lives of all people. Under this scheme, the needs of people under pressure of change become the basis for integrating one's ministry. The pastor must be several things to people:

1. *A Guarantor of Continuity.* In the midst of stress and change there is a need for someone who can "represent and guarantee a continuity with the past. It is this sense of continuity which people

desperately seek amid the confusion and chaos" of change. Radical change is undoubtedly necessary and desirable. In the midst of that change, the minister "constantly reveals the link between the present and the past." (87:34-35.)

2. *A Celebrator of Change.* Success and loss may or may not stimulate growth in individuals or communities affected by it. To celebrate change is to "honor and acknowledge" it and to give it a new perspective. Ritual becomes meaningful when seen in this light. "If successes are not celebrated, for instance, people tend to cling to past glories. If grief work does not accompany loss, a person will continue his attachment to the lost object and thus prevent new attachments and new life." (87:35.)

3. *A Negotiator of Structure.* In order to carry on his ministry to persons, the pastor must deal with the expectations of those who seek help. Traditional role expectations may be very inadequate as a framework for the helping relationship. By negotiating the structure of his relationships with people, rather than relying on outworn assumptions, the minister helps persons to adopt a more "active life style to cope with the pressures of a changing society" (87:37).

4. *A Facilitator of Meaning.* The experiences of life must be appropriated by each of us in terms that are meaningful to our understanding of who we are, what our values are, and how we understand reality. The minister relates his own values and beliefs to those of others and in their own terms helps them to make sense out of their tragedies or triumphs. (87:38.)

One is tempted to speculate regarding the impact that this type of change-oriented ministry might have in reducing the gap between change-seeking clergy and change-resisting laity. Might it not conceivably make possible a greater openness to change in the latter group and a more effective strategy for the former?

Whether or not these assumptions and perspectives on the ministry are meaningful to a particular reader, they do provide another illustration of a valuable approach to the solution of role problems. As Lee points out, these functions completely cut across traditional roles of ministry with a particular perspective. By focusing less on what the minister does and more on what impact his ministry has on the lives of people, such a perspective makes possible a unified approach to the many demands of ministry and provides a basis for establishing priorities among the excessive demands made upon most ministers.

Still another illustration of a focus for ministry comes from Reuel Howe, who analyzes different images and styles of ministry. He sees a tendency for preaching to be monological and for the clergy style of communication to be characterized by a "tell 'em and leave 'em" approach. In pastoral work he finds confusion in the minds of practitioners over the many alternative styles that they may take in their ministry. He believes that the church exists in order "to be in dialogue with the world, and the function of the pastoral, homiletical, educational and priestly ministry is to provide and maintain the dialogue between the Word of God and word of man, in order that men may know their own need and possibility, and know and accept what God has given them" (72:220). He sees the dialogical ministry as integrating all of the minister's activities, enabling him to "listen as well as speak" and to be open rather than defensive.

Be a Professional?

To focus one's ministry, then, is to guide it into channels rather than simply to allow it to develop in diffuse response to every demand or expectation of those in one's role set. It is to develop in the mind of the clergy what James Glasse has called "an image of the ministry as a whole" in distinction to the many different images of ministry that are offered him. From the standpoint of role dynamics, it may not be quite so important precisely *what* that unifying perspective is, as long as the minister has *some* unified stance.

Glasse (56) suggests that the best unifying image is that of the minister as a "professional." Some ministers will tend to dismiss the suggestion immediately because of the word he uses. To be a "professional" to many of them implies a mechanical response to people without the warm responsiveness that flows from deep commitment. But Glasse goes a long way to redeem the word and uses his definition effectively to provide a framework into which the minister can fit his various roles. The professional is:

1. *An educated man:* He is the "master of some body of knowledge."

2. *An expert man:* He is "master of some specific cluster of skills."

3. *An institutional man:* He renders service through a "historical social institution of which he is partly servant, partly master."

4. *A responsible man:* He "professes to be able to act competently in situations which require his services."

5. *A dedicated man:* He " 'professes' something, some value for society. His dedication to the values of the profession is the ultimate basis of evaluation for his service." (56:38.)

Using these categories, he illustrates with several professions such as that of medicine, for example. The doctor's education and expertise is in the practice of medicine. He serves within the context of a hospital; he is responsible to his colleagues of the medical profession to maintain a certain standard of competence; and he takes the Hippocratic oath that he will maintain an accepted ethical stance. He dedicates himself to the value of health.

The clergyman "studies theology (or divinity), practices the profession of the ministry, most commonly in and through the church" (although chaplains do so in other institutions). "He is accountable to ecclesiastical superiors, professional colleagues, and lay associates, for high standards of practice, and he labors for 'the increase among men of the love of God and Neighbor' (from Niebuhr, *The Purpose of the Church and Its Ministry.*") (56:41.)

It may be helpful here to distinguish between Glasse's concept of the minister as a professional and the use of the same term by Fichter (45). The latter conceives of the priest as being "the last generalist," and uses the word "professional" to refer to a specialized secular competence that a priest or other member of a religious order may have added to his repertoire. Thus priests may become professors, hospital administrators, or physicists, and nuns may become nurses or school administrators or teachers, etc.

Glasse, on the other hand, seeks to set a professional framework for understanding and shaping the minister's total task. To be a professional in Fichter's sense is to leave parochial work for another profession. To be a professional in Glasse's understanding is competently to fulfill a ministerial calling.

There are, of course, practical as well as theoretical limitations to the use of a pure model of the "professional" as a basis for understanding the ministry. Gannon (53) questions whether the priest/minister can be considered a professional at all, from an empirical standpoint. We cannot go into the details of his somewhat technical argument, but it is important from the perspective of this book to note one point, which he makes in various ways. A professional exercises a fairly high degree of autonomy; he operates within the framework of strong professional associations that enforce standards of performance, establish ethical expectations, and protect their rights. None of these conditions prevails for most clergy. Their status and authority are conferred upon them by organized religion and their autonomy is limited by institutional obligations. They do not have strong professional associations or colleague reference groups. The recent organization of the Academy of Parish Clergy is, at the same time, evidence of the vacuum that exists in this area and an attempt to take corrective action. (1.)

Nevertheless the professional concept, especially as Glasse has defined it, is a helpful one in attempting to deal with role overload as well as with conflicting expectations. A particularly appropriate illustration is set forth in the following passage.

One of the ways a professional assumes appropriate responsibility is by self-limitation, by not pretending to be all things to all men. If a man comes to a lawyer and says, "Counselor, I've been having a pain in my head; can you help me?" the lawyer would have to say, "That's not my kind of problem. You had better see a physician." . . .

But a man comes to a minister with almost any kind of problem and the minister says, "What can I do for you?" If a minister is a professional, he has to be a professional something. This requires that he identify those points at which his profession is to be practiced. He must make clear what he professes to know, to be able to do, through what institution, under what standards, and to what end.

Having limited his concerns to a given area of society's needs and functions, he holds himself responsible for effective efforts in that area. To be a professional in one area means precisely to be a layman in another area. (56:43–44.)

To put it another way, to hold a concept of the minister as a professional is to develop a clear rationale for specialization. If one is to focus the roles of his ministry and perhaps reduce his role overload by eliminating some of the expectations that others might otherwise have for him, he needs to have a rather clear reason for doing so. The necessity of professional specialization provides one of the clearest reasons the minister can give to his church officers and to the members of his congregation. They confront this in many other areas of life today. They can understand that, as a professional, he has a focus of competence and should not be expected to perform outside his profession, except as a layman.

Negotiate Role Changes

It should be clear by this time that the development of a focus in one's ministry, or the change of one's roles, usually requires negotiation with others. Since roles are reciprocal expectations, and involve not only the minister but also his people, and his other ecclesiastical reference points as well, he cannot arbitrarily change them. There must be a common understanding of what he is doing. We have already seen how valuable a discussion of the minister's roles can be to achieving clarification and consensus. Now we need to look a little more specifically at the process of negotiation itself.

Merton, in his work on the analysis of roles, enumerates a number of social mechanisms that operate to produce a greater degree of social order; that is, to reduce the role conflict or to "articulate" or integrate the roles in a role set. Some of these mechanisms have been mentioned elsewhere. One of them that is particularly relevant to the concept of role negotiation is the mechanism of making role conflict observable to the role senders who are involved. Merton points out that because role senders frequently are not aware of the expectations of others in the role set, they tend to operate on the unfounded assumption that their attitudes and expectations are either *uniformly shared* by others or that they are *not shared* by others at all. In either case, conflicting role demands may be known to the role receiver, but not to any of the role senders. The resolution of role conflict may then be sought by finding occasion to bring together those who are exerting incompatible role pressures in such a way that they will discover the conflicts which their expectations produce.

As long as members of the role-set are happily ignorant that their demands upon the occupants of a status are incompatible, each member may press his own case upon the status-occupants. The pattern is then many against one. But when it is made plain that the demands of some members of the role-set are in full contradiction with the demands of others members, it becomes the task of the role-set, rather than the task of the status-occupant, to resolve these contradictions, either by a struggle for exclusive power or by some degree of compromise. As the conflict becomes abundantly manifest, the pressure upon the status-occupant becomes temporarily relieved. . . . [He becomes a third party.] The status-occupant, originally at the focus of the conflict, virtually becomes a more or less influential bystander whose function it is to high-light the conflicting demands by members of his role-set and to make it a problem for them, rather than for him, to resolve *their* contradictory demands. Often enough, this serves to change the structure of the situation. (99:430–431.)

It is clear that Merton's strategy applies particularly well to situations where role senders are not aware of the conflicts they are creating. However, it might well apply to many other external role conflicts as well.

What would happen, for example, if a minister were to point out to his church officers the inherent contradictions in any particular role he was expected to perform, and if he were to ask their advice on how he should resolve the conflicts? What would happen if he involved them in the process of establishing priorities among his multitudinous responsibilities so that they could become aware of his role overload? Might they not find ways to provide needed assistance for him on the less important roles or agree to eliminating some of his responsibilities altogether? The experience of some ministers in doing this suggests it to be quite feasible. Will not responsible persons, if they have a chance to feel the problems themselves, see that the time and resources of their pastor must be allocated at least as carefully as their financial resources? Could it be that, in the resolution of role conflict or the reduction of role overload, ministers "have not, because they ask not"?

Why Be Passive?

The strategy suggested here requires an active, rather than a passive, stance. One does not solve role conflicts by waiting for something to happen. One actively explores alternative methods of reaching a satisfactory solution. One takes the initiative to get the conflict out on the table so that those whose expectations are incompatible can resolve them, either in direct negotiation with the minister, or in discussion with one another, with the minister serving as resource and helper.

Is this a natural stance for the clergyman? For some it will be. For those inclined to passivity, however, to make this approach will be much more difficult, and they will need help to do so. The skillful initiative of concerned church officers may be needed especially if it can be offered supportively.

Unfortunately, there seems to be evidence that the clergy attracts passive personalities. Schneider and Hall suggest this as one possible explanation for the passivity of Catholic priests (125:128). In a study of 25 candidates for the ministry, Whitlock found a negative correlation between passivity and high scores on the Ministry Scale of the Strong Vocational Interest Test. He suggests several possible explanations. The idealized image of the preacher may attract passive people, or passives tend to check socially acceptable answers. Also, "if the Ministry Scale was developed on the basis of organizational criteria of success, it is possible that passive persons would tend to conform to such a pattern" (145:212). Dittes observes that

the clergy role in our culture places emphasis on nurturing and succoring others, on institutional maintenance, on koinonia, peace and love, on oneness with tradition, and on the suppression of inter-group, interpersonal and intra-personal conflict. . . . There is even some reason . . . to suppose that these characteristics of a clergy role attract persons who, in some sense, have never left home except for similarly stable nurturing contexts in which oneness with the nurturing sources and controlling authority is reassuringly visible. (37:43–46.)

Certainly, all clergymen are not passive people. However, to the extent that one of them is, these suggestions may come as counsels of perfection. For others, however, the active stance in resolving conflicting expectations may make a great deal of sense. They could see perhaps how such a stance might make a difference in dealing with two of the major role problems we have described.

How can one seek a resolution to the fundamental conflict on the nature and purpose of the church and its ministry in the world, which Hadden demonstrates so forcefully? One by one, he examines alternative resolutions of the conflict, and dismisses them as unsatisfactory. Finally he comes to the conclusion that the best course of action is for the clergy to *create lay support*. By being really knowledgeable concerning the issues and by working steadfastly to bring laymen along with their understanding, the clergyman may be able to achieve some measure of agreement. To be sure, Hadden does not reflect a great deal of hope on that point, but that course of action is the only ray of hope he seems to see at all. The church is a voluntary association, he reminds us. Therefore, if its leaders have changed the rules of the game, they must either win the support of church members for the changes they have instituted or they must be prepared "to recruit new members who share their definition of the organization. Failure to achieve one or the other of these tasks will result either in the demise of the organization or their loss of the leadership role." (62:21.)

Look once more at the clergyman's administrative dilemma. This too can become the basis of negotiation, not only before a call is consummated but at any time. In fact, many ministers might be quite surprised at how readily negotiations could result in a reduction of their administrative load, perhaps through delegation of such tasks to lay leaders. Laymen may well be more ready for assignment of responsibilities on the basis of competence than ministers are. It is difficult to delegate, and few people do it well. The tendency is either to dominate, hold on to responsibilities, or to abdicate. But many laymen have to live with delegation, and are accustomed to functional accountability on the basis of specialized skills.

Still another illustration may be found in Broadus' analysis of ministerial frustrations. He describes these in terms of the minister's self-image, which conditions his *self-expectations and goals*. These, in turn, may conflict with the *expectations of others,* producing frustration. Broadus' prescription: "The minister must evaluate all expectations, both self-imposed and other-imposed, and determine a course of action. He acts, *not reacts,* to the community images. When our self-image conflicts with the community image, the minister chooses what he is to be, do and say." (23:41.) A program of self-disciplined action may include the following steps: (*a*) awareness of frustration as a problem; (*b*) identification of the cause of one's frustration; (*c*) outlining a course of action; (*d*) deciding when one will act; and (*e*) *acting.* In other words, the remedy for frustration is more likely to be discovered through planned action than through acquiescent passivity.

Everybody Wins

Two quick points about negotiation are worth making before we go farther in this discussion.

1. Negotiation of role expectations will be facilitated if members of the minister's role set respect his professional competence, and if they think he is doing a good job. Gross's study found that school board members "conformed to professional expectations" of their superintendent even when he disagreed with them, provided they respected him and put high value on his work (123:502).

2. If possible, negotiations of role conflicts should be carried on in such a way that resolutions meet the needs of all parties concerned. When somebody loses in a conflict or dispute, the seeds of later trouble have been planted. When everybody wins, it is possible to deepen the relationships of those who have been involved.

If All Else Fails

Although one has done all he can do, certain role conflicts will persist. How does one deal with them? To answer this question, it will be helpful to look at a theoretical concept called "cognitive strain," which Sarbin and Allen (123:541–543) have used in dealing with the management of role conflict.

When one receives contradictory signals from several points, such as those involved in role conflict, one delays his action long enough to understand incompatible material, weigh its meaning, and decide on a course of action. Cognitive strain is the marked increase in mental activity that occurs during such periods of indecisiveness. Two kinds of mental activity are involved: a search for more information to help in processing the conflicting data, and a search for categories into which the input may be fitted.

This increased mental activity is directed toward resolution of the conflicting situation in five alternative ways. The first of these, *"instrumental acts,"* are an attempt to modify the external situation that has caused the cognitive strain. Most of the approaches to role conflict already covered are in the instrumental category. They involve changing the role expectations, negotiating new roles, etc.

Two additional types of instrumental acts may be added to those already mentioned. First, one may segregate role conflicts by time or space. If the minister can so arrange his life as to play one of the conflicting roles at a time, so that neither role will actually interfere with the other, cognitive strain can be reduced. Sarbin and Allen give the rather unhappy illustration of the all-too-familiar man who plays the role of Christian in church, and the conflicting role of sharp businessman at the office. Ministers are not likely to respond warmly to that image, but it does make clear that roles can sometimes be insulated from one another. Presumably this does not always need to be at the cost of one's integrity.

The other form of instrumental act not yet covered is simply to escape from the conflict altogether by a drastic withdrawal. Merton speaks of "abridging the role set." One can break off certain relationships within the role set, or even leave the situation altogether. Needless to say, this will frequently be a last resort, since as a result of such action one usually will have to pay a relatively high price, enduring considerable pain, or accepting certain penalties imposed by the role senders involved.

When one is not able to use an instrumental act to reduce cognitive strain, or when attempts to do so have not eliminated the role conflict, then he has before him *four other courses of action,* which are directed more at the cognitive strain and its detrimental effects than on a resolution of the role conflict itself (123).

1. *Attention deployment* is the process by which the role occupant ignores one of the incompatible expectations in favor of the other. In a sense this is closely related to the process of role integration, which we have already discussed, but in this case one has not developed a

new or higher integrating concept that changes the roles themselves. Instead he compartmentalizes them by paying attention to the expectations involved in the role he is playing, and ignoring other contradictory expectations *at that time*.

For example, there is a conflict between the roles that the military chaplain is expected to play as a member of a military hierarchy and as a religious professional. How does he relate as a counselor to an Army private, for example, when he is an officer? Sarbin and Allen suggest that he deals with the conflict by "looking upon himself as a clergyman when operating in the context of religious service, and as a military officer when dealing with matters covered by military regulations. . . . By effective deployment of attention, incompatible inputs can be avoided by attending to other stimuli instead." (123.)

2. *Changing beliefs* relative to one or both of the incompatible role expectations is another method of dealing with cognitive strain. Again, this is similar to the integration of the minister's roles discussed earlier. However, here we stress the relative priority assigned to conflicting expectations, rather than any change in those expectations. A prime illustration comes from the study by Getzels and Guba of Air Force instructors who experienced a conflict between the expectations related to their role as teacher and those related to their role as officer.

Those who taught civilian subjects felt more conflict than those who taught military subjects; the most disturbed instructors were those least committed to military careers, and conflict was negatively correlated with quality of teaching. In both instances (the study of chaplains mentioned above and the study of Air Force teachers) the choice of the major role (officer) produced least conflict. (131:114.)

In other words, by identifying themselves with the role orientation that had the greatest pressures in a military system, teachers and chaplains were able to reduce the cognitive strain they experienced. The expectations had not changed. But their belief about the relative importance of those expectations and of who they were in relation to them, had provided a means of internal resolution of a continuing external role conflict.

Neither of the two additional courses of action from Sarbin and

Allen's analysis seems to be creative or appealing, but some people find them necessary:

3. *Tranquilizers and releasers* may ameliorate the cognitive strain. Chemicals, sleep, food, and engaging in intense muscular activity and formal games do not affect the situation itself, but they do help make it more bearable.

4. *Persistent cognitive strain* may be the price some pay for failing to find any other method of reducing the conflict. This, as we have seen from Kahn's studies, produces low job satisfaction, little confidence in the organization, and high job tension. In some cases when cognitive strain persists at a high level, illness may result.

A Word of Caution

The enumeration of a number of alternative courses of action involved in the management of role conflict may have given the impression that it is a relatively easy matter for someone to change his style of operation as a minister and simply apply one of the approaches described here, as though this were a cookbook, from which one has merely to select the appropriate recipe and follow the directions carefully. Nothing could be farther from the truth! People have their own styles of action, and whereas they can grow and modify in their understandings and in their styles, this does not happen easily or frequently, and not without considerable help. Neither has every pattern of role conflict resolution been offered here as a recommendation or as an "ideal" course of action. Each situation will require its own approach, as will each person involved.

Furthermore, many aspects of clergy role conflicts will best be dealt with by changes in the system within which the individual works. As an employment system in which considerable role conflict and ambiguity exists, it is incumbent upon the church to take whatever steps may be necessary to provide support systems of various kinds, to make necessary changes in its operation, and otherwise to assist the minister in dealing with the stresses he must face in the ordinary course of his work. Chapter 8 will deal with the organizational implications of role conflict and ambiguity.

Change the System

The underlying assumption of this book has been that the role conflicts and ambiguities of ministers are caused by many factors in their own backgrounds, in the people of their role sets, and in the institutions to which they are related professionally. Because there are complex causes, the solutions must involve the understanding and efforts not only of the clergy and of local congregations but of every part of the occupational system to which they belong.

The Church as a System

The systems approach to understanding an organization such as the church implies a concern for wholes and for the complex patterns by which parts of the whole (individuals and subsystems) interact with one another. Each unit has its discrete function, but no part can really be understood in isolation from other units, because a system is not static but dynamic. Action or change in one part of the system has impact on other parts of the system. The solution to problems within a system often involves action at more than one point in the system in order to bring about needed changes. (15.) Thus, in dealing with the incompatible expectations that impinge on the clergy, we must consider change in several different subsystems of the church at the same time if we are to effect a meaningful resolution of their problems. (65:7.) For instance, to offer career counseling opportunities without providing for corollary occupational mobility, continuing education, and other personal growth possibilities is to reduce stress at one point in the system while increasing it at several others.

Parenthetically, we note that denominations differ in the dynamics built into their systems and in the ways in which their subsystems interrelate. Although one sees dramatic and extensive recent changes, the Roman Catholic Church has traditionally come close to a pure form of bureaucracy. Its hierarchy is organized with rather clear levels of authority and with well-defined functional responsibility at each level. In fact, as Schneider and Hall (125) point out, it was the Roman Catholic Church that served as the model for Max Weber's description of bureaucracy.

Baptist churches or others with congregational polity leave much greater authority with each local congregation. These semiautonomous local churches are voluntarily joined together in associations and conventions. Thus, an effective method of solving a systems problem in the Baptist denomination will necessarily be different from a method that is useful in the Roman Catholic Church. The Presbyterian system, which involves a deliberate distribution of powers among different judicatories at several levels, in a "connectional" pattern of interlocking checks and balances, may well involve still other approaches. One must not be too quick, however, to assume that these theoretical models of church government operate as they are described.

For example, there are those who would maintain that the power of an association executive in a congregational form of government may be greater than that of some bishops in Episcopal churches when it comes to a pastor seeking to move from one congregation to another. The Baptist pastor who does not happen to have personal friends or former parishioners in other congregations is completely dependent upon the association executive, who in turn is not constrained to help him under the same defined responsibilities as those of the bishop. Personal influence becomes more important.

Whether or not that is the case, this is not the place to make a detailed analysis of the differences of church polity which need to be dealt with in making a systems approach to the role conflicts of the clergy. Suffice it to say that there are differences, that these differences are not necessarily the obvious ones, and that any proposed solution in a particular denomination needs to be developed by those who know that denomination well enough to take the real power factors, functional assignments, and systemic interrelationships into account. Therefore, any suggestions made here will necessarily be general and illustrative in nature rather than specific or definitive for any particular denomination.

Systemic Approaches to Role Conflict

There are several key points during the career of a clergyman where the denomination as a system impinges upon him. A young person is recruited, and decisions are made as to his suitability for the ministry. After preliminary acceptance, the candidate enters a seminary for his initial professional education. Along the way, he receives some form of occupational counseling, provided either formally by the church or informally by those who are his mentors. Throughout a minister's career, decisions are made regarding his assignment. These may be largely in the hands of others, as in the Roman Catholic Church, may largely be the result of a person's own entrepreneurial negotiation, or be the product of some other denominational process. There are relationships of one kind or another with colleagues and with ecclesiastical superiors. At one extreme, these may be supportive of growth and development, helping one to focus his ministry and solve his identity and role problems. At the other extreme, there may be practically no meaningful relationship at all. There are structures of church government and planning that may liberate a person for his ministry, channel it and make it fruitful, or thwart and frustrate it. They may create role problems by expecting the unreasonable and by failing to take adequate steps in the direction of clarity, or they may facilitate role clarity and the resolution of role problems that do arise. (65:7-8.)

All these areas of career impingement on the clergy suggest different points at which the system can attack the problems of role conflict and ambiguity. They will be dealt with in more or less the order indicated in the above paragraph. Interestingly, these areas of concern relate closely to suggestions that Kahn (76:387) makes as to ways in which the incidence of role conflict and ambiguity may be reduced and damage to the person or organization minimized. (For our purpose here, Kahn's categories have been rearranged. Our categories have been indicated in parentheses.)

1. *Introducing new criteria of selection and placement.* (Recruitment and placement.)
2. *Increasing the tolerance and coping ability of individuals.* (Career counseling, education, and training.)
3. *Strengthening the interpersonal bonds among organizational members.* (Supporting communities.)
4. *Introducing structural changes into organizations.* (Structural changes, parish development consultants, goal-setting and performance review.)

Realistic Recruiting

In view of the number of unpleasant surprises that seem to prevail among many new ministers regarding role demands made on them in their first parish, the church needs to concentrate careful attention on helping candidates for the ministry to acquire a realistic picture of the roles they will be expected to fill. For instance, unless and until there can be a significant change in the emphasis that congregations place upon administrative activity, candidates should prepare themselves emotionally and with needed skills to be administrators as well as preachers and pastors. They should realize they are not likely to have as much time for scholarly pursuits as they might like.

Criteria for the selection of candidates for the ministry should take these factors into account. A careful look might also be taken at whether in fact the ministry does attract passive persons, and studies might determine whether or not that is desirable in view of the demands that the clergy must face.

Careful attention needs to be given to the interface between the judicatories that hold legal responsibility for ordaining the clergy and seminaries that prepare them. While technically the former recruit and select ministers, it appears that more active and organized recruiting is done by seminaries than by judicatories, and that their selection process actually determines those who enter the ministry much more frequently than most churchmen are ready to admit. If institutions staffed by people who have given their lives to scholarly pursuits select ministers for the pastorate, are they not more likely to select those who excel as scholars and who draw back from administrative responsibilities? Should not active pastors exercise more vigorous responsibility for recruiting and selecting candidates before they are admitted to seminaries? One realizes that this may be a counsel of perfection at a time when increasing numbers of seminary students enroll before they have made any decision on whether or not they want to seek ordination.

Normative Career Counseling

It is clear that career counseling is one of the critical services that must be available to the clergy at periodic intervals throughout their service. This should be mandatory before candidates are accepted initially by their judicatories and prior to their entering seminary. Before ordination and before accepting calls to first pastorates, candidates might seek further career counseling, to give them deeper insight into themselves in relation to the specific role pressures they can anticipate in their first charges.

Henderson found in his counseling with prospective candidates for the ministry, at the Northeast Career Center, that special attention needs to be paid to the realism factor in counseling with prospective candidates.

Although theology enters into the picture in the counseling of every client, it is of particular importance with candidates or prospective candidates. This is usually most apparent when there is a consideration of the role of the minister and the role of the church. There can be a discrepancy between the person's understanding of himself and society as over against his understanding of the Christian, the minister, and the church. Stereotypes—many of them contrary to what generally exists—are common and usually monolithic. Realism and the possibility of pluralism can be introduced. (69:2.)

A number of earlier references to the work of career counseling have made clear the value of such a service in helping the minister know more clearly who he is, what he has to contribute as a clergyman, how he can focus his ministry, etc. Brown points out that more than 80 percent of the clients of the Northeast Career Center come because of their confusion over their role and purpose. Williams, of the Midwest Career Center, puts the clarification of role confusion at the top of his list of client needs.

Brown states several principles of the career center process that facilitate the clarification of identity and roles.

> Career counseling for ministers should be conducted in a setting and in a manner that recognizes the theological and ecclesiological context in which ministers make decisions about occupation.

> Career counseling for ministers should utilize acceptable and proven behavioral science disciplines in the practice of counseling. . . . Donald E. Super's self-concept developmental theory of vocational choice and Ginzberg's theory of integrative compromise as essential to occupational decision-making have provided the framework for the techniques and instruments used at the Center. . . .

> Career counseling for ministers should contribute to the development of capacity for self-management and self-actualization by clients. (25: 35–37.)

Preparation and Readiness for Ministry

As has already been emphasized, churches and seminaries must give more careful attention to ensuring for ministers the type of preparation that will enable them to deal with the administrative and organizational role demands that are made on them. Practical courses in management, delegation, sensitivity training, group process, management of change, supervision, goal-setting and review are needed.

Experiments should be conducted to determine at what point in a young minister's career these skills can best be acquired. To what extent should they be included in the seminary curriculum? In an intern year experience? In some form of residency or continuing education program during the first years in a parish? More attention needs to be given to establishing patterns of supervision, which, as in the social work profession, will be normative during the whole training period and will be carried over into professional practice, with supervision gradually changing to a consultant relationship as a person matures in the ministry. Helen Irvine has suggested that this kind of relationship needs to be established by the candidates' committee of a judicatory, during the middler year of seminary, in order to determine how a candidate is performing in his seminary field work. Such a process should include goal-setting for the work and for personal growth as well as periodic reviews of the extent to which goals have been reached. This, in turn, should be followed by the setting of new goals as the cyclical process starts over again. The discussion of role theory, the analysis of expectations, etc., might be more meaningful if it came in this context than if such knowledge came at any other time or in any other way. A good experience with meaningful supervision can help young pastors discover the value of supervision both for themselves and for those they may supervise. The habit of setting goals can give a sense of direction they might otherwise miss. To learn how to be responsible for the work of others may help reduce one of the causes of role conflict. (76:381.)

It is clear from the research on stress in the ministry already cited that the critical period of transition from seminary to the practice of ministry requires much more careful attention than has yet been given it. One therefore welcomes the efforts being made to determine criteria for the assessment of readiness for the ministry. Such a study has been undertaken by a task force of the American Association of Theological Seminaries. Preliminary work has identified four characteristics that seem to be necessary in a young minister, four "turn-off qualities" that hinder his success, and eleven "minimum abilities to begin ministry." (103.) As these are further developed, they may prove helpful in the selection and preparation of ministers. More important from a systems standpoint, however, is the analysis of four subsystems that interact with one another and with the ministers' personal and professional qualifications. These subsystems are:

1. The seminary faculty and other sources of ideal or conceptual models of ministry;

2. The various denominational persons responsible for "brokering" placement, career development resources, and other opportunities for the local minister;

3. Professional peers in the ministry, including the spectra of different generations and denominations; and

4. The lay "market" whom the pastor will serve both in his own congregation and in the larger community with which he works. (103:3.)

Somehow, ways must be found for these four systems to work together more closely if the bridge between preparation and practice is to be negotiated more effectively by young ministers. One effort in that direction that seems to have exciting possibilities is an experiment with a completely new approach to theological education that is under way in Washington, D.C., under the auspices of the Metropolitan Ecumenical Training Center (involving sixteen Protestant, Jewish, and Roman Catholic jurisdictions and agencies). The aim is to provide theological education within the context of the work of ministry rather than in a seminary, and to integrate theological education with lifelong continuing education. Called "Inter-Met," for the interfaith metropolitan approach that it seeks to implement, it provides a structure within which students (after screening by their denominations for the ministry) go to work in some project in the greater Washington area. Each student relates to an on-the-job training committee in his work, and to a core group of other students who develop supportive relationships for worship, feedback, and exploration of problems in relation to religious heritage. A college of preceptors provides potential courses in a wide range of subjects to be taught under "field conditions" after a contract for teaching of the course has been negotiated by the student with the preceptor. The student pays for the preceptor from his job earnings. A staff facilitates the process, and a review committee evaluates contracts and the program as a whole. At the outset, each student works out with the staff an individually tailored educational plan, prepared in the form of a contract.

The first year of this unique program concentrates on the practice of ministry, on personal growth (in a group with a psychologist and a religious teacher), and on political and social issues (in a group with an expert in political life and a religious teacher). The theologue learns during that period to identify his needs, set his goals, "negotiate for the agendas of these groups with the money he is earning," etc. As the prospectus puts it:

After a person has been in the process for the first phase, he might have gotten a clearer picture of (1) the human issues of his job: its problems and possibilities, (2) his own way of working and the effects he has on others, and (3) the society and community problems within which the

religious communities work. Also, he and his colleagues might have be-
gun to form ideas about what they need to know in order to do their
jobs satisfactorily and, where needed, how to attempt to re-define the ministry so that it may be used to meet human needs. (46:9.)

By the end of the first year, students are expected to have identified
their needs in concrete terms and then are expected to pursue their
programs through similar contract arrangements for a total period
of work and study that the sponsors anticipate will not take less than
two years, nor more than five.

Programs such as Inter-Met are not likely to meet the *volume*
needs for the preparation of ministers, so one must look to the
seminaries to meet the challenge.

Fortunately, seminaries are beginning to demonstrate a growing
awareness of the need for radical changes in theological education.
Many are engaged in significant experiments. The level III program
of the San Francisco Theological Seminary, leading to the M.Div.
degree, is an example of an effort to go beyond the traditional field
work approach and provide for more intensive and extended involvement in ministry under supervision and in combination with seminars, group discussion, and other approaches to the analysis of
ministerial roles. Such experiments need to be encouraged and should
somehow bring into a close working partnership the four subsystems
identified above.

Placement

One of the most crucial areas of needed action is to develop placement systems that will ensure that before calling a pastor, each congregation will have carefully thought through what it is trying to do,
what it expects of a minister, and what kind of minister can fulfill
those expectations. (96:2.) Ministers need to go through a similar
process of clarifying their own expectations for ministry and of
identifying clearly what kinds of role demands they are willing to
meet.

The Department of Ministerial Relations of the United Presbyterian Church, which provides a dossier service on available ministers

to judicatories and churches, now requires that before being eligible to receive dossiers, the session of a church must fill out a church information form. In addition to factual data on the congregation and on the community, this asks them to provide an analysis of the significant problems and issues confronting them, a description of the ministry they are carrying on *to their members,* the ministry they are carrying on *beyond the church membership,* and their mission goals and objectives. They are asked what skills, abilities, and types of leadership are needed *from the congregation* to carry out their mission, and what skills, abilities, types of training and experience they need *in a pastor.* Where possible, the supplying of this information is to be preceded by a careful study process involving the people of the congregation in understanding their situation and the meaning of the church's mission in it. (21.)

The Lutheran Church in America, which is participating in the Church Manpower System (mentioned previously), is developing a pastor-matching program which is called Personnel Support Services. It seeks information from congregations similar to that mentioned above, but does so in categories that precisely match those which clergy use in registering for placement.

In addition to gathering the usual personnel data asked of ministers, the Church Manpower System asks the minister to indicate which six of the fifteen functional areas (Table 7 in Chapter 5) represent his areas of greatest competence. The registrant gives information on his training, experience, and degree of skill in up to thirty different skill areas, and elaborates on his style of working with people, of exercising leadership, of planning, programming, and evaluating. Ministers summarize their theological orientation and their feelings about community action, etc. All this is recorded in such a way that a rough computer match of a registrant's pattern of ministry can be made with information supplied by vacant congregations.

Congregations, through their boards, describe in fairly concrete terms what the attitude of their people is toward change, toward initiative on the part of their membership or of the clergy, toward various types of ministerial leadership, and toward community action, etc. Using the same categories that the clergy use, they assign priorities to the fifteen functional areas of ministry. This is preceded by a congregational planning process that projects congregational goals for a five-year period.

The previous pastor of the vacant congregation prepares a report in which he comments on the strengths of the congregation, their primary problems and weaknesses, and the changes he has observed in their lives and ministries. He enumerates their major opportunities for ministry and (again making use of the same fifteen functional categories) gives his rating of the priority needs of the congregation as well as a rating of the emphasis of his own ministry.

In response to actions by the National Council of Catholic Bishops in 1968, the Center for Applied Research in the Apostolate (CARA) has developed a national personnel sharing program with a central job bank. Through this clearinghouse, the bishops may seek personnel offered by other bishops and religious orders. A process of "corporate decision-making" includes analysis and classification of the job demands, vocational self-appraisal by individuals, and placement after an analysis of the match between the two. (82:98–102.) Similarly, The Episcopal Church has established a Clergy Deployment Office, which also makes use of the Church Manpower System.

The Synod of Minnesota of the United Presbyterian Church is experimenting with relocation seminars to help pastors understand what is involved in moving to another parish or in finding secular jobs. Through lectures, discussion, role-playing, and other group processes, participants are helped to develop their skills in dossier preparation and in interview participation. Leadership includes representatives of the denomination's Department of Ministerial Relations, personnel directors from industry, the director of a career guidance center, and others.

Without going into further detail on other programs or procedures, we may observe that the hopeful sign in these denomination-wide moves is found in their recognition that both pastor and people must think through and share with each other in advance of establishing a relationship exactly what their goals and expectations are. In these and other instances, denominations are putting their weight behind procedures that will stimulate a good deal of careful thinking, generate increased information, and ensure communication of this data in both directions. If carefully employed, such procedures should go a long way toward developing a common understanding of the expectations of each and toward minimizing unnecessary role conflict or ambiguity.

Supporting Communities and Continuing Education

As has been suggested, one of the ways in which role conflict and ambiguity may be reduced and damage to the person or organization minimized is through the "strengthening of interpersonal bonds among organizational members." This has important implications for the creation by the church of increased opportunities for clergy and lay leaders to meet together for extended periods of time to think together about the mission of the church and their mutual responsibility in it. The plea by Maier, mentioned earlier, which grew out of the Nature of the Ministry seminars, needs to be taken very seriously. How can communication channels be improved unless those who need to communicate with one another begin to spend time in retreats, talking and listening, thinking together, reading the same books and periodicals, having some of the same experiences? Where is this being done on any large scale today?

A variant of the principle just referred to is given by Merton. He affirms that one way to deal with role conflict problems is to develop social support by others in similar positions with similar role difficulties. A natural answer for the clergyman, of course, would seem to be for him to find such support among his fellow clergy. Theoretically presbyteries, associations, or district conferences provide the context within which such mutuality can thrive.

Actually, the sense of a true colleague relationship seems to be very largely missing. Undoubtedly there are experiences of such fellowship in ministerial associations and in some informal study groups that arise here and there. But the evidence is discouraging. Supporting communities of ministerial colleagues simply do not exist in any significant numbers. The Episcopal study (43) found that the "parish priest has little satisfying contact with fellow Episcopal clergymen. Of 14 work-related activities that were rated in terms of satisfaction, the priests were most dissatisfied with the companionship of other Episcopal clergymen." The Temporary Commission on Continuing Education of the United Presbyterian Church reported that more than half of the ministers studied had experienced a crisis of faith at some point. Of these, 83 percent reported that they had not felt free to discuss their problem with anyone, so had handled the crisis alone. The loneliness of the ministry cries out from such figures. Mills found in ministers who left the pastorate for secular work a high proportion who felt professionally alienated from their colleagues, "having no close friends among fellow ministers and not feeling well accepted among them" (101:112).

Jud's study of ex-pastors also revealed that the support structures of the church did not sustain them. What help they did receive came from outside the church, drawing them out of the pastorate rather than confirming them in it. They felt that the help they needed simply was not there when they needed it. With alarm, the authors observe that pastors' views about the church's support system were like those of ex-pastors. (74:53.)

An important additional dimension to our understanding of a minister's support structure emerges from the recent study by Mills and Koval, which is entitled *Stress in the Ministry*. When asked what steps they took to help ease their stress, two thirds of the respondents said that they took independent action and did not seek the help of others. This is consistent with the loneliness already described above. One third did seek the help of colleagues, wives, superiors, etc. Surprisingly enough, however, when asked who was most helpful to them in resolving their stress, only 5 percent responded "no one." One third of the respondents mention their wives and 40 percent name colleagues or superiors as important in helping them. (106:28–29.) In other words, although a clear majority of ministers try to resolve stress on their own, a very high percentage of them find that their actual help comes from others.

"In the light of evidence of alienation and isolation between ministers, the prominence of colleague support in these findings is somewhat surprising," the authors comment. "Part of the explanation must be that the support system we have just described reflects help received rather than actually sought. . . . The barriers between clergy may only come down drastically when melted from the outside in a time of need." (106:36–37.)

Here is a clue of bright promise. Clergy do not see their colleagues as helpful in general or as a group, nor do they seek help from them. But they *are* willing and able to receive help from particular colleagues whom they respect or who are close to them. Therefore, as Mills and Koval suggest, "what is needed is more structured opportunity for supportive relationships to develop and for news of another's need to be heard by colleagues" (106:56).

The time to begin this process is clearly as early as possible in a minister's career. As has already been made clear, the period of greatest stress in the ministry is the first few years after ordination. From some recent research, it would also appear that this is potentially the period of greatest opportunity for helpful continuing education. Hesser and Mills (70) found a significant correlation between high levels of stress and expressed need for continuing education. The early parish years are a period of high stress. We could, therefore, anticipate at that time a genuine openness to growth through continuing education. On the other hand, the study found little relationship between expressed need for continuing education and actual participation in continuing education events. Expressed need, we are reminded, may be thwarted by lack of funds, lack of time, or both. This seems to be confirmed by the further finding that availability of time and money for continuing education is significantly related to participation in study programs. In other words, where there is high stress and expressed need, the provision of time and money should result in high levels of participation in continuing education programs.

These findings all underline the importance of such programs as the Young Pastors Seminars of the United Presbyterian Board of Christian Education and the Young Pastors Pilot Project of The United Methodist Church.

Three years after graduation from seminary, every young Presbyterian pastor is invited to spend several days with other young pastors who graduated when he did. They have an opportunity, in a retreat-like atmosphere, to live, study, and think together about their ministries. The sharing of disillusionment, of success and failure, of doubt and uncertainty, in the presence of several resource persons with expertise in the ministry, in group work and in counseling, is a deeply meaningful experience to many a pastor. The opportunity is repeated each year for a total of three years. Wives participate in the second and third years.

While similar in a number of ways to the above program, the

Methodist Young Pastors Pilot Project was somewhat more structured in its approach than is the United Presbyterian program. (122.) Cluster groups were organized consisting of from 5 to 8 young pastors, three to five years out of seminary, who lived close enough to one another to get together readily. Each group met once or twice a month on professional and personal development with an experienced fellow pastor whom the group had selected as a "pastoral associate." He was considered to be neither a teacher nor a supervisor but rather an enabler and working model of the professional practice of ministry. Pastoral associates met together every six weeks for training sessions designed to help in their special assignment. An important by-product was the development of a colleague support relationship with other experienced ministers not unlike that which developed with the young pastors in their clusters. Three- or four-day seminars of all young pastors and pastoral associates were held at the beginning, midway, and at the end of the two-year experimental program. They focused particularly on three areas: (*a*) human relations, (*b*) Biblical and theological understandings, and (*c*) social issues.

From Competition to Colleague Cooperation

The establishment of meaningful colleague relationships for the clergy will require careful thought and considerable experimentation. There appear to be elements of competition that normally enter into the relationships of one minister with another. This is particularly true within the structures of a church court, in which colleagues may vote for or against another's proposition and may help or hinder his goals if he exposes himself too openly to them. In a profession that places so much stress on humility and even on self-effacement, this may seem a strange phenomenon. Perhaps as Dittes (37:43–46) has theorized, one can understand the minister in terms of the emphasis which the church has given to "community" in contrast to "agency." Dittes defines "agency" as the striving to enhance individuality. He suggests that because feelings of agency have been relatively subdued (more latent than manifest), they are all the more powerful. Perhaps it is the latent feelings of agency in the context of assumed community that operate to prevent open sharing among many clergymen with their fellows. While professing community, they have strong needs to assert individuality.

On the other hand, some interesting experiments are in progress which suggest that, under the right conditions and with skilled leadership, it is possible to develop communities of mutual support among clergymen. Robert Worley tells of his work with clusters of Roman Catholic and Lutheran clergymen in Chicago, who have been meeting together for a number of months, exploring how to be colleagues. They come together in groups of 13 or 14 for two and a half hours on Monday mornings to share in a process of problem-oriented continuing education and skill development related to the practice of ministry. Meeting initially once a week for assessment of their ministry, they gather every three or four weeks with such high commitment to one another that all absenteeism is carefully accounted for in advance of each meeting.

The Albany Synod of the Reformed Church in America has initiated a support system for the clergy that aims to deal comprehensively with their needs. The initial step was the holding of two series of pilot Vocational Development Workshops. One group of pastors was gathered from rural, suburban, and urban communities in a wide geographical area across New York State. Another group was made up of pastors serving small rural congregations within several miles of each other. It is hoped that the latter group will use the Vocational Development Workshop as a first step in the building of a supporting community of ministry. (134.) Wives were invited to participate. Initially each group of about a dozen people met with three professional consultants for two days. Tests and other instruments, developed for career counseling of the clergy, were administered to analyze their abilities and identify their concerns. About a month later the groups met again for a day to discuss the findings of the first session and to explore with each other their particular capabilities. After another month had elapsed, a third day was set aside for participants to plan personal programs of vocational development and continuing education.

In addition to the obvious purposes of this program in the area of group career counseling, the evaluation report speaks of renewed commitment to the ministry, and of a "new sense of mutual support" among ministers, their wives, and fellow ministers.

A major effort at collegial clergy professional development on a national scale is the Academy of Parish Clergy, Inc. This professional organization focuses on study and growth by practicing pastors, through colleague relationships with fellow clergy and with the laity. Each member undertakes a minimum of 150 hours of continuing professional education each three years, evenly divided between work done in the parish and away from the parish. There are regional workshops and an annual meeting in which research and case studies are analyzed. The Academy, as its brochure announces, seeks to provide ministers with "the support and challenge of peers" and to fill their need for "an association in which to establish discipline, set standards, enhance competence, develop clear images, and experience esprit de corps."

An important emphasis of the Academy is collegiality (6). Members of the Academy undertake to engage fellow clergy in a process of mutual learning regarding their practice of ministry. Colleagues meet periodically to share their firsthand experience of the ministry (3). One method, for example, is to select several *tellers* who, in about eight or ten minutes, *describe* their own experience in some particular aspect of the work of the minister (5). *Askers* probe the experience of the tellers in order to clarify what is actually happening. They press for justification of the style or course of action taken by the tellers. A process observer sees that the ground rules are obeyed and helps the group to see more clearly how they are functioning as a group. Observers ensure, for example, that tellers do not use *prescriptive* language (which tells what *ought to be*) but use *descriptive* language to tell what *is*. Askers are not allowed to make speeches or to frame leading questions. They must inquire and probe and seek additional description. Thus it is hoped that members will develop the skills necessary to learn from each other.

Henry Adams, director of the Academy, believes deeply in the necessity of collegial groups. He points out that, as a professional, the minister must satisfy expectations of both customers and colleagues. "The tensions thus imposed are both important and psychically demanding. Most clergy try to be professional without any system which is conducive to a style of life in which accountability to peers (support and challenge) is a significant part. So they are aspiring to the impossible."

Colleague teams can be formed, not only with fellow clergymen, but with other professionals as well. For example, Fr. Gerald O'Bee in Rochester, Michigan, has set up a cabinet of laymen, mostly professionals with their wives. They see themselves as all in the teamwork of ministry together. Each agrees to confirm and challenge the rest as may be necessary for their "growth in the corporate ministry they share." Together they make plans and evaluate the work they have done. "Reduction of role conflicts takes place as a function of the practice of the profession. Sometimes those lay-peers occupy the 'consumer role' and sometimes the 'peer role.' . . . The real issue is how to structure relations so that . . . week after week the work of ministry is carried on within collegial frameworks that are enabling."

In Minnesota a group of ministers meets monthly "to set mutual goals, criticize each other's goals and study together." They have decided to "form a group of consultant specialists, each man of the group utilizing his continuing education study leave to develop his expertise and capabilities in a given specialty such as, small group work, Christian education, stewardship, youth work, etc."

Just as support groups can develop at their own initiative around concerns for growth and continuing education, so it is possible for seminaries or other institutions to initiate programs that meet these same needs. The Hartford Seminary Foundation (66) has decided to give up its historic task of preparing ministers in a B.D. program and has decided instead to concentrate its resources in a four-fold approach to (*a*) career planning and professional development; (*b*) parish renewal consultation; (*c*) ministry studies research; and (*d*) extension service overseas in the first three areas.

The proposed program for *career planning and professional development* is unique in that it reverses many of the roles usually played by an academic institution. Emphasis is upon dealing with the needs of ministers and congregations in the midst of the situations where they work, rather than within the classroom.

The plan is to form working groups of about fifteen ministers in the same area. The ministers themselves will plan and operate the programs, setting their own agendas and schedules. The seminary will assist them in securing the outside professional resources they themselves have identified as necessary. A coordinator will serve as liaison between the work groups and the seminary staff. While the seminary will provide part of the leadership cost, participants must help find some of the funds before the program will be initiated.

The feasibility of this program has been tested through small informal meetings with ministers in New England. The response has been "sober but enthusiastic." Groups outlined priority needs such as "professional identity and role," "renewal of personal faith," "updating Biblical and theological knowledge," "professional skills in counseling," and relating "the Christian faith to personal and social problems." (66:3.)

The Interdenominational Theological Center in Atlanta has identified particular needs for the continuing education of black clergy and is instituting a process of several steps for meeting those needs. A four-week resident program at the Center in Atlanta will concentrate on five skill areas: (a) *communication;* (b) *leadership skills* (including "organizational development, planning, decision-making, conflict management and team building"); (c) *pastoral skills;* (d) *sociological skills* (including exposure to communities, "plunge type experiences, simulation games," etc.); and (e) *theological skills* (exercised within the context of life situations such as night courts, emergency waiting rooms, food distribution centers, and the like).

At the conclusion of the resident program, participants will set goals for their work in back-home situations during the subsequent year. The staff will then visit periodically with participants in their working communities and will hold one-week follow-up "Personal Growth Seminars" for groups of these participants. These seminars will focus on "a broader understanding of Church problems and community issues," acquainting participants with "simple research tools, public and private resources, techniques and strategies currently being employed to cope with them." An annual assembly is projected to help all participants become "aware of their collective strength and potential" and "to encourage them to think of national impact and effect as well as local." (73:13–17.)

Structural Changes

Two recurring themes in our analysis of role conflict have been the minister's distaste for administration and the need for more effective communication of role expectations. Both of these problems can be helped by certain structural changes in the system to which the clergy relate.

"Clustering" is a new pattern of church organization by which several neighboring churches, often of different denominations, voluntarily join together under a common board and with a joint or united staff. Usually the process of developing a cluster involves a good deal of self-study on the part of each congregation, and this, of course, facilitates a clearer understanding of why the church is there and what its members are trying to accomplish. (39.)

A uniting of the staffs of several churches makes it possible to specialize. One minister who is particularly good at Christian education may take that responsibility for all congregations, or another who is an effective administrator may carry the administrative load, etc. A sense of collegiality in the ministry and the discovery of a new sense of purpose by both clergy and people often result. When this happens, there is a clear possibility of a locally based support system in which staff members with different abilities complement the several ministries of the others and provide for mutual challenge, encouragement, and growth.

The "clustering" principle suggests that several smaller churches might join together to employ a lay administrator who could handle many of the administrative responsibilities that otherwise take up the pastors' time.

Still another type of structural modification, which is being tried experimentally in a Roman Catholic parish in Stockton, California, involves an attempt to give each priest within the parish the full range of pastoral responsibilities that normally are reserved to the pastor himself. The parish is divided into districts, with an associate pastor in charge of each district. His task is to provide all the pastoral functions for that district. The whole parish is coordinated by a pastoral board. (82:104.)

Beyond the national structures mentioned in the discussion of placement concerns, there is a need for additional structures at the judicatory and local church level. An increasing number of local churches have found it helpful to have a personnel committee (of perhaps three to five members) to study the goals and priorities of the congregation, draw up descriptions of accountability, work with staff on their own related goals, review their fulfillment of these objectives, conduct an annual performance review, ensure appropriate continuing education opportunities, be available to staff for consultation and advice, conduct annual compensation reviews, and engage in other such activities.

James Little, of the Lafayette-Orinda United Presbyterian Church, Lafayette, California, has developed with his church officers a small executive committee, which meets with him frequently throughout the year to act as his "supervisor" and to "keep him honest." Each year at the organizing meeting of the session, a series of secret ballots are taken. The elder who first receives a majority of votes becomes the clerk of session. The next two who receive a majority vote are the other members of the executive committee. Together with the pastor, they set the goals for his work, review the record he keeps of the way he spends his time, and otherwise provide him with guidance on the fulfillment of his ministry.

At the judicatory or area level, there is a growing trend toward the assignment of full-time staff to the concerns of the clergy.

Since 1968, the Rev. Glenn E. Matthew has been serving as superintendent of ministries for the Kansas Area of The United Methodist Church. Recognizing a need for support structures in addition to the regular administrative guidance provided by bishops and district superintendents in the Methodist system, Bishop Stowe assigned Matthew the task of developing a support system for ministers "from decision to death." Included are such functions as recruitment, preparation, counseling services, pastoral care of ministers, career development, continuing education, performance evaluation, and working closely with district superintendents as they fulfill their responsibilities.

Several judicatories in the area around Kansas City, Missouri, have developed a judicatory career support system, which includes provision for career assessment, organizational consultation, continuing education, in-service training, church oversight visits, and performance appraisal. (112 and 140.) Eugene Timmons, director of the program, feels that the integrated approach to these diverse elements provides opportunity for judicatories to take the initiative in expressing their concern for their pastors in flexible ways not possible when these functions are dealt with separately.

In 1971, a director of personnel was employed by the Presbytery of New York to assist its ministers and congregations in placement, to ensure adequate resources for career counseling and other help to pastors, to develop performance review procedures, to encourage continuing education opportunities, to devise procedures for annual compensation reviews, to work on salary standards, to recommend adequate benefit provisions and pension coverage, and to work with judicatory committees on all matters of personnel concern for the clergy and for other employed personnel. Whereas small judicatories may not be able to afford the cost of this kind of staffing arrangement, larger ones certainly can do so, or programs can be worked out on a regional basis. Properly carried out, such provision should help greatly to minimize role conflicts and their cost.

Parish Organizational Consultants

Another alternative that is becoming increasingly popular is the employment of parish consultants who have specialized skills in organizational development. Congregations or pastors may call upon their services as needed to help solve parish problems. Anderson, who has been serving as director of parish development in the Episcopal Diocese of Washington, writes of needed changes in church systems.

I believe that one such essential change is to make it practical and normative for clergy to have professional assistance available *within the congregational setting* in order to assist with the development of adequate role descriptions and procedures. (9:9.)

He describes, in an excellent brief article on clergy role development, some of the ways in which such a consultant can help the parish priest, and the congregation as a whole, to face conflicts that develop, through helping them to diagnose and work through the nature of their problems.

In view of the complexity of role conflict and ambiguity, expert assistance at critical points may be the only solution to the problems inherent in some pastorates. Toward that end, The Episcopal Church has been involved in Project Test Pattern, an experiment that has resulted in a network of seventy-eight project consultants and forty-one parishes who have entered into contracts for their services.

A summary evaluation with several case studies is entitled *New Hope for Congregations* (94). In one parish, for example, the rector asked a consultant to lead a conference to clarify his role as rector. A series of meetings with the vestry, the rector, and the consultant, led to the conclusion that part of the problem was the rector's own confusion about his task. He was encouraged to go through the career evaluation process at the Northeast Career Center. In addition, it became clear that the vestry needed to improve its patterns of communication and to develop better methods for dealing with conflicts. An objective and skilled third party was able to help them deal with these needs.

In another parish, a series of meetings of the congregation, the trustees, and the vestry helped identify a number of structural and group process problems involving the leadership style of the rector, inadequate decision-making mechanisms, lack of clear goals, inadequate structures for planning, etc.

As a result of a number of such pilot experiences, Project Test Pattern has concluded that congregations can change and that "third-party consultation can increase the rate and effectiveness of change."

Largely as a result of the demonstrated effectiveness of the Project Test Pattern program, The Hartford Seminary Foundation (as mentioned above) plans to include in its services to congregations the provision of consultant services in its Parish Renewal program.

The Lutheran Church in America is involved in a Parish Life Development program, which seeks to develop consultants with basic organizational development skills to be located in their different synods, so that they can then work in local congregations. Congregations, in turn, select Parish Renewal Teams, who are trained by synod consultants to work on situational analysis, the formulation of congregational goals, the identifying of available resources, and program planning.

Early in the program, two things have become clear: (*a*) It is difficult to give volunteer consultants sufficient training to make possible their performance at high levels of competence. (*b*) Organizational development work at the congregational level inevitably raises issues that must be dealt with at the synodical and denominational level. Here is another illustration of the truth that one cannot work with a subsystem in isolation from the whole system. Accordingly, the Lutheran Church in America has initiated experiments with several synods to help them with various organizational processes, including programs of goal-setting and review.

Church-related organizational consultants in different parts of the country are finding their services much in demand, so it would appear that this approach to the reduction of role conflict might be an idea whose time has come.

Goal-Setting and Review

There remains one approach of major importance. Once the baseline for the congregation's role expectations of the minister has been established at the time of his call, the most effective way for pastor and people to grow closer to one another in their understanding of their common calling is regularly and systematically to plan together and periodically to review their progress toward mutually agreed upon goals. Such processes can provide the minister with the feedback he so much needs if he is to grow in his understanding of his calling and in his effectiveness in fulfilling it. A number of different approaches to this will be suggested in Part III.

PART III

GOAL-SETTING AND REVIEW

So far, we have discussed the reduction of clergy role conflict and ambiguity through action that the minister *himself* can take and through changes that the church as a *system* can make in relating to him at various points in his career.

There remains one important area of consideration that deserves careful development, not only because of its high potential for the creative management of role conflict but because it involves an arena of action that is just beginning to receive the attention within the church that it deserves.

The remaining chapters deal with various processes of communication that organizations use for establishing work goals, clarifying responsibilities, measuring accomplishments, and planning professional growth. We refer to such processes under the broad-gauge heading of "Goal-Setting and Review," even though, to be technically accurate, the title would need to be much more complex.

It will be quickly recognized that industry has had a great deal of experience and has been involved in some research related to the subjects with which we are dealing. Professional associations, government agencies, and nonprofit organizations have also been concerned with these matters. (32, 40, 75, 90, 100, 107, 120, 139, and 144.) The church can learn a great deal from these different sources, but none of them is likely to provide ready-made approaches that are directly applicable to the needs of the church and its clergy. The church must discover methods of its own that are uniquely suited to its needs. Fortunately, there are several experiments in progress—

some quite creative—that may provide clues for the development of future patterns. It is hoped that by making some of them more widely known, pastors or people who would like to move ahead in these areas will be encouraged to do so. Therefore, illustrations will be taken largely from actual programs that have been tried in the church, although possibilities from other sources will also be suggested. This makes no pretense at being a comprehensive collection of possibilities for goal-setting and review, but does hope to take a first step in encouraging others to share what they are doing.

CHAPTER 9

Where Are We Going
and How Am I Doing?

Goal-setting and performance review can be important tools for the pastor who desires to be more effective in his ministry. If carried out in cooperation with leaders of his congregation, with colleagues and with other expert resources, such planning and stocktaking can improve the working relations of the pastor by keeping open his channels of communication with his people and enabling him to focus his ministry.

A Desperate Need

This study has made it abundantly clear that solutions to role conflicts and ambiguities of the clergyman will be discovered in the area of improved communication between the minister and the members of his role set. A quick recapitulation of some major points will remind us of this:

1. Clergy and laity frequently have differing understandings of what the minister ought to do.
2. Clergy perceptions of the expectations of their lay leaders have been shown to be inadequate in many cases. There is a great need for dialogue so that laymen and ministers can understand each other.
3. Discussion of clergy roles has proved to be an effective method of bringing lay leaders and ministers closer together. It is important to make role conflicts visible so they can be dealt with.
4. In the face of role conflict or ambiguity, people tend to with-

Summary of first part of book.

draw rather than increase their efforts to communicate. This only makes matters worse.

5. An active stance on the part of the clergy, rather than passivity, is needed if role conflict is to be reduced. For those ministers who are inclined toward passivity this may be difficult.

6. There is an urgent need for dialogue on the goal and purpose of the church's existence. Some of the confusion and disagreements that exist cut deeply into the effectiveness of the church. Lay and clergy leaders alike owe it to their people to discover where the church should be going. The complexities of the present age do not make this easy, but it must be done!

If there were no other reason for doing so, the urgency of mission issues in our day would in themselves justify the spending of considerable time in planning and in establishing effective continuous channels of communication between ministers and people. But there are other reasons as well.

Am I Going Anywhere?

Goals are important to the minister. Without a clear sense of purpose, doubt may debilitate him or he may discover to his amazement that he is merely drifting. Effectiveness requires a working relationship with a host of individuals and groups. On what basis does he decide on his priorities if he has not first asked, "Where am I going, and what do I want to do when I get there?"

It appears that many effective ministers do spend a good deal of time planning for the work of their churches with their church officers and in setting priorities for their ministry. But the need for goal-setting is not as obvious to most clergy as one might suppose.

Of the clients of the Midwest Career Center, 54 percent "lack a sense of goal-directedness," according to Frank Williams, the director. Most have "never allowed themselves to think in terms of career goals" (146:8) because this would imply they were being "ambitious" or were not relying on the Holy Spirit. Others have never considered the possibility that goal-setting might provide a tool that would enhance their effectiveness in the ministry. "One of the most consistent items of feedback to the Center from former clients is appreciation expressed for enabling them to set reasonable goals and to strive toward them in their ministry."

In apparent contrast to this, Mills observes:

Few ministers seem to work on the model of the "settled pastor" of old; i.e., patiently doing the ministerial routine and keeping the church year steadily turning in harmony with the ebb and flow of life. A pastorate is seen more as *a project—a sequence of goal-conception, planning, organization and achievement.* On this model a man often gets restless when the sequence is completed and his work becomes routine. He either begins again with new commitments and new goals or decides that it is time to move. (101:151; italics mine.)

Actually, there is more consistency between these two findings than is immediately evident. There is a difference between "career goals" and the immediate and tangible goals that are set in a working situation. The minister who comes to a parish that is greatly in need of Christian education facilities, for example, may bend every effort toward the task of galvanizing the congregation to action. Once he has raised the funds, planned the building, and seen it to completion, he may feel that his work has been accomplished. He is ready to move on. Indeed, it may be necessary for him to do so.

He has been setting short-range goals for his work, whether or not he recognizes them as such. He may never have determined any long-range goals, either for the congregation he serves or for his ministry. He may even be opposed to doing so. Such goal-setting as takes place may be done almost subconsciously, and with a great deal of vagueness, and without involving others in his congregation. It may even arise, somewhat fortuitously, out of a series of events in the life of the church that thrust him into the position of leading a building program.

The need that is being underlined here is for a more conscious, careful, and concrete setting of goals that are informed by a knowledge of the minister's calling, his particular gifts, and the congregation's sense of mission within its particular constellation of opportunities and problems. Certainly, the Holy Spirit does not have to be excluded from such a process!

How Am I Doing?

The minister needs some basis for assessing what is actually happening as a result of his ministry. He may tell himself that this is unnecessary, since he is fundamentally accountable to God for *faithfulness* and not for *results*. Although he may find Biblical support for this position, he must also recognize in his ministry the calling to equip the people of God for the exercise of their ministry in the world. In this task, effectiveness is not easily divorced from faithfulness. The two dimensions are certainly not identical, but neither are they completely separable.

Furthermore, the experience of both the Northeast Career Center and the Midwest Career Center seems to underline the human need of ministers to evaluate their ministry. Thomas Brown says that the major question asked by his clients is, "How am I doing?" Similarly, Frank Williams finds recurring dissatisfaction among his clients because, with limited feedback from others, they find it difficult to know whether or not they are doing anything meaningful. Another counselor who has considerable experience with church personnel believes that one of the deep longings of the minister is for a feeling of competency. This, of course, involves questions of preparation, specialization, role clarification, etc., but it also relates fundamentally to the minister's need for the right kind of feedback on the value of his ministry to his people. Reference has already been made (Chapter 3) to the way in which lack of adequate feedback on the performance of the priest was found by Schneider and Hall to hamper the self-actualization of Roman Catholic priests.

All of this is part of the same picture, the implications of which perhaps can best be summarized by the words of one pastor of the United Church of Christ who had left his work in the parish. When asked what advice he would give to lay leaders of the church, he wrote:

Good advice

> Develop criteria and methods for periodic review and evaluation of (1) specific congregational goals and emphases, and (2) the effectiveness of your pastor in fulfilling his role in reference to the accepted goals and emphases. Develop ways of communicating official appreciation for services rendered. Find out ways of hammering out congregational priorities together with the pastor so that the pastor and official board are working as a team in pursuing the accepted goals. (74:8.)

In 1971 the Academy of Parish Clergy appointed a task force to study "The Appropriate Self-interest of the Profession." A survey asked Academy members to identify their "most vital concerns." Henry Adams writes that the Task Force "expected members to talk about salaries, job security, information about pastor-eating congregations, etc. To their amazement, respondents placed two needs way ahead of any others: . . . help in evaluating professional performance, and help in working better with laymen." Of course the two are closely related.

Why Doesn't More of It Happen?

If the need for goal-setting and feedback is so apparent to counselors and researchers, why do not more pastors and congregations make use of these tools?

Perhaps, for one thing, it is because many ministers are not fully aware of the possibilities. As one denominational executive put it, "Most pastors are not aware of the technique, are not familiar with the concepts, and seem reluctant to institute goal-setting." There is the traditional individuality of the clergyman and a tendency toward entrepreneurship, which is coupled with the idea that a minister as an individual is called of God, and responsible only to him. Furthermore, the idea of performance review can be threatening. While wanting feedback, the minister readily recognizes the dangers of a process which, if not carefully conducted, can easily become judgmental rather than helpful in its net result.

In addition, even when the minister is convinced of the value of goal-setting and review, his church officers may not be. One pastor speaks for others when he says: "The thing that has been the greatest difficulty I have had is a reluctance on the part of officers to actually evaluate what I am doing. They frequently maintain that they are not equipped to do an evaluation of this kind, though many of them do it in their own businesses and professions all the time." Albert L. Haversat, of the Lutheran Church in America, thinks the reaction of lay leaders to performance review of their minister is a dual one. On the one hand, they feel that it must be done. On the other hand they exclaim, "How dare we evaluate him?"

One would hypothesize that there may be many reasons for such a reaction. Lay leaders may be reluctant to use performance review programs, knowing the problems such programs have had in industry, and recognizing that these programs are not directly applicable to a profession such as the ministry, where there is no supervisor-subordinate relationship. But more important, if their pastor is really the one to whom they go as a spiritual adviser in relation to matters of deep personal concern and of eternal as well as temporal import, it would be strange indeed if they were not hesitant about being put in a position where they would seem to sit in judgment on his effectiveness. The parallel with the patient-doctor relationship naturally suggests itself. In the presence of family or friends, a patient may not hesitate to criticize his doctor. However, if he really wants an evaluation of the doctor's professional competence, he will turn to another professional. He dare not trust his lay judgment if he has any genuine doubts about the surgeon who holds his life in his hands.

One pastor, who has encouraged the evaluation of his work by his church officers, feels that the hesitation they express arises out of "a real gulf between the work of a layman and the work of a clergyman." He feels that if "we can overcome this with an understanding of laymen as, indeed, themselves ministers of Christ, and the professional ministry as simply one form of a broader ministry . . . there may be more willingness to look helpfully at the work of the pastor."

Perhaps encompassing all these reasons is a lack of clear formulation of how goal-setting and performance review applies to the work of a minister and of his congregation. To move forward in this area, it is important that the following steps be taken.

1. Know the possibilities of goal-setting and review;
2. Clarify the purpose of employing these processes in the church;
3. Agree on who the minister is and how these techniques relate to him; and
4. Decide on the type of criteria that need to be used.

These are the matters to be discussed in Chapter 10.

A Quick Look at Goal-Setting and Review

Before examining specific approaches to goal-setting and review in the parish, we shall take a quick look at the issues involved in applying these methods to the church. In general, models for these functions that are relevant to the minister and his work come either from the *professions* or from *organizations* such as industry, government, nonprofit agencies, the military, etc.

Organizational Models

Performance review in its basic form comes from industry. An employee and his manager are involved in periodic appraisals of his performance. Peter Drucker says: "To appraise a subordinate and his performance is part of the manager's job. Indeed, unless he does the appraising himself he cannot adequately discharge his responsibility for assisting and teaching his subordinates. Nor can he adequately discharge his responsibility to the company for putting the right man in the job." (41:150.)

Many different plans for performance appraisal have been developed over the years. In general they are designed to meet three needs:

1. They provide systematic judgments to back up salary increases, promotions, transfers, and sometimes demotions or terminations.

2. They are a means of telling a subordinate how he is doing, and suggesting needed changes in his behavior, attitudes, skills, or job knowledge; they let him know "where he stands" with the boss.

3. They also are being increasingly used as a basis for the coaching and counseling of the individual by the superior. (144:71.)

Job Descriptions or Accountabilities?

Usually appraisals are based upon an assessment of the effectiveness with which an employee is performing the duties of his job. In that connection it may help to distinguish between a job description and a statement of accountabilities. A detailed description of the activities a worker is expected to carry out we call a *job description*. For a worker who is involved in *routine* duties, the job description may provide a meaningful base for evaluating his work, especially if it is accompanied with a statement of the standards of performance which he is expected to maintain, or a description of the way in which he must carry out his tasks if performance is to be considered satisfactory. (75:6–7.)

A statement of *accountabilities* may be distinguished from a job description in that it emphasizes the *end results* that the worker is expected to achieve rather than the tasks he is expected to perform. Applied to the minister, a job description might say that he "visits the sick in the hospital" whereas a statement of accountabilities might say that he "meets the spiritual needs of the members in time of crisis." The latter is obviously a statement that allows considerably more discretion to the worker. Therefore, a statement of accountabilities is more appropriate to higher-level workers, since it does not attempt to spell out *how* the worker carries out his work, but indicates instead what the desired goal of his work may be.

As Levinson points out, job descriptions tend to be static, and "the more complex the task and the more flexible a man must be in it, the less any fixed statement of job elements will fit what he does. Thus, the higher a man rises in an organization and the more varied and subtle his work, the more difficult it is to pin down objectives that represent more than a fraction of his effort." (89:126–127.)

We may pause to observe that two important difficulties in applying organizational methods to the minister's task have already emerged: (*a*) He does not have a supervisor-subordinate relationship, and (*b*) the subtleties of his work make it exceedingly difficult to define clearly what results should be expected of him.

Performance Rating

Among the most common or basic methods of performance appraisal is that in which the superior, once or twice a year, is required to rate his subordinate on various scales provided for him. These may include the skill with which the employee carries out his duties, his relationships with fellow workers, personal qualities, etc. The supervisor is required to discuss his ratings with the subordinate and to make suggestions on ways in which he can improve his performance. This, incidentally, is one point where performance appraisals often fall down. Supervisors are reluctant to conduct the performance interview. In addition to rating scales (which may take many different forms), narrative descriptions may be employed in the reports, which in turn may be used as a basis for various personnel actions including wage and salary administration and promotion. As will be seen, there are numerous pitfalls in this kind of process. Readers who wish to study performance evaluation will find several helpful works listed in the bibliography. (32, 40, 75, 90, 100, 107, 120, 139, and 144.)

Performance Appraisal Is of Questionable Value

Several years ago, the General Electric Company conducted an extensive research project to study the value of their performance appraisal program. They had observed employee defensiveness and manager resistance to the process, and were uncertain as to whether or not they were accomplishing their purpose—namely, to improve the performance of their workers. As a result of the study they concluded that "a detailed and comprehensive annual appraisal of a subordinate's performance by his manager is decidedly of questionable value. Furthermore, as is certainly the case when the major objective of such a discussion is to motivate the subordinate to improve his performance, the traditional appraisal interview does not do the job." (100:124.)

In more detail General Electric's findings included the following:

Criticism has a negative effect on achievement of goals.
Praise has little effect one way or the other.
Performance improves most when specific goals are established.

Defensiveness resulting from critical appraisal produces inferior performance.

X Coaching should be a day-to-day, not a once-a-year activity.

X Mutual goal-setting, not criticism, improves performance.

X Interviews designed primarily to improve a man's performance should not at the same time weigh his salary or promotion in the balance.

Participation by the employee in the goal-setting procedure helps produce favorable results. (100:124.)

Goal-Setting and Review

As a result of these studies the General Electric Company separated their salary appraisal program and salary discussions from their efforts to improve performance. In place of the traditional performance appraisal approach, they initiated a Work Planning and Review program (WP&R) in which manager and subordinate are expected to meet together much more frequently. During these meetings, "progress on past goals is reviewed, solutions are sought for job-related problems, and new goals are established." Emphasis is placed on the setting of mutual goals and on problem-solving rather than on evaluation. In fact, no ratings are made. "The intent of the method is to create a situation in which manager and subordinate can discuss job performance and needed improvements in detail without the subordinate becoming defensive." (100:128.) Further studies showed that much greater improvement of performance was recorded by this mutual goal-setting and review process than by the old method. Meyer reports:

Goal-setting, not criticism, should be used to improve performance. One of the most significant findings in our experiment was the fact that far superior results were observed when the manager and the man together set specific goals to be achieved, rather than merely discussed needed improvement. Frequent reviews of progress provide natural opportunities for discussing means of improving performance as needs occur, and these reviews are far less threatening than the annual appraisal and salary review discussions." (100:127.)

Management by Objectives

Another variation of the plan just described is even more widely known and practiced. In essence, this calls for goal-setting by the employee in consultation with his superior, coupled with self-evaluation and coaching by the superior. Again this is in contrast to an "evaluation," which seems to connote something done to the employee, or an "appraisal," which implies a *judgment* passed upon him.

The management-by-objectives model involves a cyclical planning process that might be outlined for an "employee" with a supervisor as follows:

1. The employee defines his accountabilities: prepares a draft proposal, discusses it with his manager, and revises the draft to their mutual agreement.

2. The employee sets goals for his work in the light of the overall objectives of the organization and of his accountabilities, prepares proposals that he discusses with his supervisor, and revises in the light of the discussion.

3. Frequent reviews of the employee's progress toward his objectives are held with the supervisor. They consider accomplishments and obstacles preventing accomplishment and make plans together for corrective action he may take.

4. Annual or semiannual review of progress toward goals establishes the basis for setting new goals:
   a. The employee prepares a self-evaluation.
   b. His manager does the same.
   c. They meet to discuss the self-evaluation and to prepare revised goals as a starting point for the next cycle.

As McGregor points out, an approach such as this emphasizes analysis rather than appraisal. The supervisor serves less as a judge and more as a coach, doing that for which he is best fitted: helping the employee relate his self-appraisal and personal goals to the "needs and realities of the organization. . . . In the discussions the boss can use his knowledge of the organization to help the subordinate establish targets and methods of achieving them which will (*a*) lead to increased knowledge and skill, (*b*) contribute to organizational objectives, and (*c*) test the subordinate's appraisal of himself." (144:75.)

It will readily be seen that this approach includes a high level of participation by the employee at every step in the process, and that, in line with the concerns of Levinson, the personal goals of the subject are related to the goals of the organization.

Professional Models

Performance evaluation for the *professional* is quite a different process from that for the *employee.* Usually the professional has no supervisor to whom he reports. He does, however, have professional colleagues who are equipped to assess the effectiveness of his practice, his skill, and his knowledge. (1.) Henry Adams has stated:

> The professional is part of a community of professional peers to whom he exposes his techniques and knowledge and who interact to upgrade themselves. [He] finds his evaluation chiefly among his colleagues within his profession, who know best what resources available for service have or have not been employed. . . . In the final analysis, only professional colleagues know enough to evaluate professional performance. . . . They support and challenge, keep men honest, accept responsibility for mutual discipline, and set standards for each other. (7:103–104.)

Who Is the Minister?

We have already observed that in the clergyman's unique situation no single approach to goal-setting and review is directly applicable. We need now to look more clearly at the methods that will be applicable to him. To do so it is important first of all to answer rather clearly *who* he is, *to whom* he is accountable and *for what*.

Henry Adams suggests that there are two possibilities. A minister may be either a *professional* or a *technician*. The technician may be as highly educated as the professional, but differs from him in that he puts himself "under the tutelage of superiors," adopting what they test and refine. The professional, on the other hand, is continually reflecting on his practice, deriving theory from it, refining that theory and using it to determine what he does in his practice. As has been indicated above, he also brings himself under the careful scrutiny of his colleagues in the profession, with whom he joins in the formulation and enforcing of professional standards for his practice.

Employee or Autonomous Professional?

To carry the distinction a step farther, we may ask if the clergyman is an *employee* of his congregation (which pays his salary) or if he is an *autonomous professional* who serves the congregation on a retainer fee. To think of him as an "employee" implies a degree of subjection to an employer (supervising board of trustees, or congregation), which seems to underlie some proposals for reviewing the minister's work. The employer, it is reasoned, should supervise the employee. This is hardly likely to be well received by most clergymen as an adequate description of their status or of their relationship to the congregation they serve.

To speak of the minister as an autonomous professional will probably be much more congenial to the theology and self-consciousness of many ministers. Again, however, this is an inadequate description of the relationship that the minister must have to his congregation and to his board, session, or consistory. He is indeed a professional, but he does not have an individual practice in the same sense as do other professionals, such as doctors or lawyers. He has an organizational type of accountability that makes him different from other professionals.

A Minister-Director?

If the minister is neither employee nor autonomous professional, what is he? Presumably his relationship falls somewhere between these two extremes. The particular polity under which a minister serves may make a good deal of difference as to which of the poles is more nearly correct.

Perhaps the terms "minister-director," "minister-executive," or "minister-manager" come as close as any designations we can find to covering the clergyman's identity and relationships. In many respects he is a professional whose service can adequately be evaluated only by fellow professional colleagues or, as Adams suggests, by colleagues (both lay officers and clergy). At the same time, he has organizational responsibilities that are intimately involved in his calling, and he is accountable for organizational results, which makes the pure form of professional accountability to peers a very inadequate operational picture. If as a professional he sets his own goals and maintains professional standards without regard to the program goals of the congregation he serves or the judicatory to which he belongs, he will inevitably increase the chasm between his own expectations for ministry and those of others. In fact, the use of such a model by many clergymen may indeed be responsible for much of the role conflict that exists today. The minister cannot simply be an autonomous professional who serves a group of people as he may see fit, without regard for their expectations. But neither can he be a mere technician, nor an employee who is subject to their every wish and to goals that they may set without reference to his professional competence and ecclesiastical calling.

He is, then, a professional with dual accountability: to himself and his professional colleagues on the one hand, and to the community of God's people or the organism of the church on the other. He is, if you will, a professional who serves the community and is organically accountable to it.

A Minister's Accountabilities

As will be seen from Table 10, each of these alternative interpretations of the minister's identity has implications for the nature of his accountability. If he is an employee, he should be guided basically by the desires of his employer, who works with him to prepare his job description or list of accountabilities and to whose organizational goals he is subject.

The autonomous professional, on the other hand, is accountable primarily for meeting certain professional standards of both qualitative and quantitative nature and for a continuous process of professional development relating to those standards. Organizational concerns are quite secondary.

If, as has been suggested, the clergyman is a professional who is accountable to the organic church, then goal-setting and review must somehow take both institutional and professional factors into ac-

Table 10

THE NATURE OF THE CLERGYMAN'S ACCOUNTABILITY

WHO IS HE?	TO WHOM IS HE ACCOUNTABLE?	FOR WHAT IS HE ACCOUNTABLE?
Employee or Technician	To his "employer": Local church officers, Congregation	Job description, Accountabilities, Organizational goals
Autonomous Professional	Himself, and Professional colleagues (both lay and clergy)	Professional standards — qualitative performance — quantitative performance, Professional development
Minister-Director	Judicatory, Local church officers, Himself, Professional colleagues (both lay and clergy)	Organizational goals — program end results, Accountabilities, Professional standards, Professional development

X

count. It is clear that organizational goals are not necessarily identical with the goals of the clergyman for his own ministry. Nevertheless, each must be informed by the other, and an effective and fruitful ministry must discover ways in which they creatively interrelate. Individual and institutional objectives proceed along parallel paths. In fact, as has been suggested, it seems reasonable to suppose that some of the role conflict problems that have been identified earlier in this study arise because many ministers operate on the professional track without placing sufficient emphasis upon, or building bridges to, the organizational track. Goal-setting and review, then, must deal with both dimensions of ministry and, if successful in creatively interrelating them, may help reduce role conflict and ambiguity.

One dare not close this chapter without adding a third dimension to the picture of the minister's accountabilities. For many, this would be the first line of accountability they would consider, and one that conditions the other two. It is, of course, the vertical sense of divine imperative . . . the call and purpose of God . . . the Good News . . . the Lord with us . . . the Spirit of God . . . the Word of life and truth. However a particular minister may phrase it, whatever his particular theological perspective, for most there will be that sense of Otherness which transcends the organization of the church and the professional expertise he may have acquired. God has called. Having responded to that call, the minister has an ultimate allegiance to divine expectations, which challenge all other expectations. The servant of God then must at the same time sharpen his sensitivity and obedience to that inner voice, while making certain he is not using his transcendent accountability as an escape either from rigorous professional integrity or from dynamic organizational responsiveness.

CHAPTER 11

How Ministers Get Feedback

Specific applications of goal-setting and review to the work of the clergy will be examined systematically in the next three chapters. This chapter will look at approaches that secure feedback either for the minister himself or for the minister and the board with which he works. Whereas incidental aspects of goal-setting may be involved in some of the methods described here, the primary emphasis is on performance review or on securing information on which a man may base efforts to improve his ministry.

Chapter 12 will go on to describe methods that more consciously involve the minister and his board in the setting of goals for his ministry and for the work of the church. Again, there may be elements of performance review in them, but their primary focus is upon setting goals and measuring progress toward reaching them. Chapter 13 will describe an approach that combines some of the elements of goal-setting and performance review with professional development counseling, within the local parish setting.

How to Read These Chapters

Illustrations given here have been gathered from many sources and are not necessarily set forth as models of goal-setting and review. Some of these methods would not be recommended by the author. They have been included in order to report the range of patterns that have been used in the church and to illustrate some of the pitfalls as well as the possibilities involved, in the hope that they will be suggestive of other approaches that can be tried. In each case the reader will wish to weigh the applicability to his situation of any ideas found here.

These three chapters will be most helpful if they are considered in the light of the insights of Chapter 10 and with a good deal of imagination. Thus an approach outlined here, which in itself may not be at all usable to the reader, may trigger in his thinking a completely different pattern that will meet his needs quite well.

In looking at each illustration the reader may wish to weigh what would happen if the particular elements involved were to be modified, either as to method or as to the person or group that is participating in the evaluation. For example, when an illustration describes an evaluation carried on by a *personnel committee,* consider what difference it would make if the same process were carried on by one of the following persons or groups:

A representative of the larger judicatory
A group of ministerial colleagues
A layman from outside the congregation, who is a personnel expert
A minister consultant from another conference, presbytery, or denomination
Some other independent third party serving as consultant
The entire board or session
All of the local church officers
A retreat of interested members of the congregation.

Or, as another illustration, when a method described here speaks of *data-gathering* by *informal conversation,* consider what difference there would be if that method were to be modified by gathering data—

by the use of a rating scale
by open-ended descriptive questions
by group discussion
by the use of a self-evaluation instrument
by a combination of these.

Similarly, other elements in programs that have been tried may be modified in some way, or combined with the insights of other programs in order to get the specific approach that is most likely to meet the needs of a particular situation.

Focus on the Pastor's Work

Methods of securing feedback may be grouped into those which evaluate the pastor's work, those which involve professional consultation, and those which focus on program evaluation. The first group is most closely related to industrial performance appraisal, particularly in its more formal manifestations.

1. *Informal and Personal Discussion with a Trusted Confidant.* This is the "safest," most informal, and least conspicuous way in which a minister can secure feedback on his work. A trusted layman or a fellow pastor may serve as a sounding board or counselor. In some cases, field staff members of national agencies, who do not have direct administrative relationship with a pastor, may serve this function. Even judicatory executives find themselves involved in "informal, personal, rather subjective job performance work by way of conversations and visits," as one of them puts it.

2. *Informal Discussion with a Personnel Committee.* This method is used in some churches, particularly larger ones with multiple staffs. Often such a personnel committee reviews salaries and consults with the ministers and staff members in drawing up their job descriptions or accountabilities.

Thomas Gillespie, of Burlingame, California, reports on the procedure followed by the personnel committee of his church:

The method employed for the annual review with each staff member is an informal personal interview. No instruments other than personal conversation are used. The committee meets prior to the interview and discusses each staff member on the basis of personal observation and "input" from others in the congregation in a strictly informal manner. The interview is relaxed, candid and, in my experience, generally helpful. It provides me with an honest "feedback" from responsible members of the congregation. . . .

The program here is a good one, primarily because of the high caliber of people who serve on the committee. This year, for example, Mr. "X" (a professional management psychologist) is the chairman. His professional experience and insights enhance the quality of the review and evaluation. The weakness of any such program, it seems to me, is the highly subjective character of such an evaluation. However, the absence of any objective criteria makes subjectivism difficult to avoid.

The user of such a procedure should of course consider what differences might be introduced if a personnel committee were to employ other methods of data-gathering, etc.

In line with this open-ended approach are the recommendations of the Washington Episcopal Clergy Association (143) that "every clergyman request an annual evaluation and discussion of his work with the vestry (or the person or board to whom he is responsible)." Its description of the purposes of such an evaluation is suggestive:

1. To provide the clergyman with a more accurate picture of how his congregation (or employer) sees him than he might receive informally.

2. To allow the minister to express his opinions about how well the Vestry (or Board) has fulfilled its responsibilities to him.

3. To establish goals for the work of the parish in the coming year.

4. To isolate areas of conflict or disappointment which have not received adequate attention and may be adversely affecting working relationships.

5. To clarify expectations on both sides which will help put future conflicts in a manageable form.

6. To provide an additional and valuable factor for the Vestry (or Board) to use in setting future compensation. (143.)

3. *Performance Rating.* At the other end of the spectrum of approaches to evaluation is the use of a rather highly structured performance rating form that is weighted to reflect the relative importance of activities in which the minister engages. One such form was developed by an industrial psychologist who worked with the Presbytery of Indianapolis (UPCUSA). (117 and 118.) A list of activities and attributes is placed in the first column. This includes administration, church education, church finance, community activities, continued education, counseling, evangelism, general attitude, pastoral calling, preaching, etc. A second column asks for the assignment of a percentage to indicate the relative weight or importance of each activity or rating. Thus if preaching is twice as important as pastoral calling, it might be assigned 20 percent,

whereas calling would have a weighting of 10 percent. The percentages assigned to all activities should total 100 percent.

When evaluation takes place, each activity is assigned a number from 1 to 5 to indicate the performance rating decided upon. 5 = outstanding progress; 4 = above-average progress; 3 = average progress; 2 = below-average progress; and 1 = unsatisfactory progress. The rating is placed in a third column. Multiplying the rating by the percentage figure gives a weighted score for each activity. This is placed in the fourth column. A total score can easily be computed by adding all these separate scores.

A simple, unweighted rating form was used by the Presbytery of Monmouth (UPCUSA) in New Jersey from 1969 to 1971 on an experimental basis. (149.) Also adapted from industrial patterns, it provides for a summary rating on a four-point scale (outstanding, excellent, average, unsatisfactory), and for narrative replies to *Job Description, Evaluation of Performance,* and *Comments by Reviewed Individual.* The minister is rated on:

Characteristics: knowledge of work, preaching ability, teaching ability, planning and organizing ability, initiative, development of personnel, work results, counseling ability, visitation, conducting of worship, and other characteristics to fit the particular church.

Qualities: leadership ability, cooperation, judgment, personality, creative ability, and other characteristics to fit the church.

Each of the characteristics and qualities is listed on a separate line. Opposite each, the rating form provides a row of twelve boxes for rating on a twelve-point scale. Three boxes are provided for "outstanding," three for "excellent," three for "average," and three for "unsatisfactory." Attached to the form is a description of performance rating levels, which sets forth in a sentence or two what each rating level means. (See Appendix 1.) As will readily be recognized by those with experience in rating processes, definitions such as this increase the accuracy of ratings, since raters are using a common definition.

As part of the original process, it was suggested that there be a review of the pastor's salary, largely on a comparative basis with salaries of others who work in public school administration, middle management, and neighboring pastorates. In addition, both sessions and pastors were asked to set goals for the coming year and a single-page questionnaire asked, *"Is a gap developing between the congregation and the pastor?"* Under this, other questions included: "What is the issue involved? When did it start to develop? How big is it? Is it getting larger or smaller? What effect is it having on the congregation? On the pastor?" Also requested were "Suggestions for bridging the gap."

As one might expect, the use of these materials was not wholly successful. Reference has been made earlier in this book to conclusions from General Electric research that performance evaluation ratings tend to generate resistance at various levels, and do not improve performance, and that salary review should be separated from performance review. In addition, one would speculate that the question regarding possible gaps between pastor and session might readily be misinterpreted by ministers or church officers as being investigative rather than supportive in intent.

In any case, as Paul Sobel, presbytery executive, reports, the initial approach outlined here met with a "varying amount of success and 'flak.'" The process encountered increasing resistance from ministers, and finally after an evaluation, was abandoned in favor of a new approach that was more descriptive and less judgmental, one that sought to take into account the "integral relationship between the pastor's performance and the session's performance."

4. *Descriptive Evaluations of Pastor and Session.* In order to minimize some of the threat involved in their rating procedures just described, the Presbytery of Monmouth developed a new form that no longer uses rating scales on the minister's characteristics and qualities but instead focuses more attention on the pastor's *work* itself and the way he does it. The personnel commission of a congregation is to work with the pastor in enumerating the "things to be done" by him and in describing the criteria by which his performance will be judged in the performance review.

"Things to Be Done" are listed under three general categories: (1) preaching, teaching, and the conduct of worship; (2) pastoral care (visitation, counseling, personal relations in group activities);

and (3) administration (planning, organizing, personnel, leadership).

"Performance Criteria" are to be written up in advance opposite each of the above activities as follows: (1) contents and presentation, (2) extent of calling and intention, and (3) staff work expected of the pastor. More will be said later about the establishing of performance criteria.

In the "Review" process, two kinds of reactions are sought: (1) "Appreciations," and (2) "Possible Improvements." These appear in a third column so that they may be compared with the related expectations.

In like manner and at the same time, the session is asked to enumerate at the beginning of each year its areas of responsibility in terms of (1) activities; (2) goals for the year; (3) relationships; and (4) performance criteria. At the end of the year, when the pastor's work is reviewed, the session's performance is also reviewed, making use of the same four categories.

5. *Summary of Effectiveness and Planning for Improvement.* James W. Muir, of Willingboro, New Jersey, developed a plan of performance appraisal with his church officers which made use of three open-ended questions (111):

1. Areas in which the minister's work is *most effective.*
2. Areas in which the minister's work is *satisfactory.*
3. Areas in which the minister's work *needs improvement.*

Each year, the church's personnel committee meets with the minister. Several weeks before the meeting, copies of the form are filled out by the five committee members and by the minister himself as a tool in self-appraisal. The chairman summarizes replies from committee members and adds the minister's self-evaluations, clearly marked as such. This summary, distributed in advance of the meeting, serves as basis for a discussion, leading to the formulation of a "Plan for Improvement." A summary of the discussion is reported by the personnel committee chairman to the session at the time it conducts its annual review of the terms of the minister's call. The pastor makes a practice of leaving the meeting during that report, and then answers questions growing out of it when he returns to the meeting.

Muir reports his own feelings about the process:

Having participated in four such evaluations, I can testify that the discussion and comments have always been thoughtful, honest, frank, but always in a spirit of love. In such a context, defensiveness, whether on the part of the committee members or minister, is rare, although on occasion it has occurred. It must be recognized, however, that such defensiveness is sometimes a natural reaction so no one gets unduly upset by this.

Muir finds a number of advantages to the process. It is (*a*) a means of systematic evaluation of the minister; (*b*) a source of justifiable criticism of the minister's labors; (*c*) an opportunity for him to receive confirmation of his effectiveness in certain areas, with corresponding "ego satisfaction"; (*d*) a check on the realism of his own self-evaluations; and (*e*) a means of opening the officers to a discussion of the mission of the church. He points out that:

After the first performance appraisal was held, the personnel committee made twelve recommendations to the session, all of which were accepted, each dealing with the session's involvement in mission. The implementation of these recommendations greatly strengthened the church and gave the elders a clearer understanding of their responsibility to bear rule in the church.

The Consultation Model

In contrast to the approaches enumerated thus far, other methods of evaluation emphasize the autonomous professional character of the clergyman's task and place their stress upon the minister's obligation to engage in self-generated activities of consultation with specialists in ministry. He organizes peers and laymen into teams with whom he consults about his work. By drawing upon the insights of members of his consulting team as they interact with him, the minister can draw conclusions regarding the effectiveness of his performance and engage in a continuing dialogue with others who help him improve the quality of his ministry. (1, 4.) Henry Adams writes:

In Lakewood, Ohio . . . Jack Hart has each year organized teams of officers and laymen to explore with him the form, direction and effectiveness of his ministry. The first such effort focused around the question, "How can I discover what people hear in my sermons without jeopardizing our common worship?" . . . So effective was it for all concerned that a second exploration was proposed: "What ought people to be hearing in the sermons?" This was deferred to a later year in favor of the question, "How can we make worship peculiarly our own, using the experiences and insights of members of the congregation?" Aside from the evident contribution to clinical learning for this mature and experienced pastor, the effort was proved a form of ministry in itself, increasing the laymen's awareness of their roles and their competence for it. (8:4.)

Measurement Against Professional Standards

One of the assumptions underlying all performance review is that criteria can be established as bases for the measurement of effectiveness or that professional standards can be identified against which the professional and his colleagues can evaluate their work. Without explicit and objective criteria, performance evaluation is highly subjective, unless of course it involves measurement of progress toward predetermined and measurable goals. We may observe in passing that other professions use descriptive standards as a means of measuring performance.

In the Veterans Administration, for example, the work of a Rehabilitation Counselor is evaluated qualitatively by whether or not certain functional results are evident in the handling of cases. (172.) It is considered that effective rehabilitation counseling must include all of the following:

1. Determining the counselee's vocational and related problems and needs, especially in relation to his disability;

2. Developing personal information (with the counselee) that will contribute to the solution of his vocational adjustment problems;

3. Appraising (with the counselee) vocational possibilities and helping him select and plan for the achievement of vocational objectives;

4. Certain qualitative interviewing attitudes and skills, consulta-

tion with other professionals, referrals, maintaining adequate records, etc.

Each of these functions in turn can be described in greater detail through several subfunctions which have been identified. A supervisor who has this detailed analysis of effective rehabilitation counseling clearly in mind can examine interview reports, tape recordings of interviews, and his own exit interviews with clients, in order to make some judgment on the counselor's professional strengths and weaknesses. This will give the supervisor a basis for suggesting ways in which the counselor may improve his professional skills. Thus professional standards, set forth clearly and in detail, can provide an important tool for the improvement of the skill of vocational counselors.

It may be helpful at this juncture to point out that performance criteria can be developed by preparing for each function or end result a statement that begins with the words "Performance is satisfactory when . . ." The balance of the sentence is framed so as to describe the specific types or qualities of activity or end results expected. For example, one such statement might be, "Preaching is satisfactory when sermons are well-organized, reflect study, and deal with a variety of timely and relevant subjects." In his *Standards for Executive Performance,* Wyn Gilbert (54) groups standards into three different types (with respect to measurement). There are *qualitative standards,* which consist of intangibles not reducible to statistics. These could usually be descriptive in their formulation. *Verifiable standards* are those that are neither definitely statistical nor entirely qualitative. For example, to be "regular in attendance" might be such a standard. *Quantitative standards* are, as their name suggests, measurable or countable. They may be expressed in percentages or in whole numbers of some kind.

Pastors and church officers who wish to develop standards as basis for review of clergy performance will find it helpful to reread previous chapters that analyze the different clergy roles and to study the statement on "Competence in the Parish Ministry" adopted by the Academy of Parish Clergy (Appendix 2). One pastor (47) took these standards as the basis for a series of questions on which he secured ratings on his ministry from the leadership of his church. In addition to this statement, another helpful tool is found in Appendix 3: "Guidelines for Using the Pastoral Performance Record."

If a subsequent step is anticipated, one in which evaluation of performance will take place against standards that have been agreed upon, a helpful format is suggested in Appendix 4. Note that in that scheme the evaluation process consists of examining each job segment in terms of the performance standards that have been agreed upon in advance, indicating whether or not performance meets standard or has been above or below standard. In each case, supporting evidence of the evaluation rating is given by describing specific results.

After each job segment is evaluated, a summary is prepared indicating high achievement areas and areas where improvement is needed. This in turn provides the basis for a discussion in which an improvement plan may be developed.

Focus on Program Evaluation

Many ministers and their boards draw back from direct performance appraisal and instead use approaches that are less personal and more programmatic. While these may have the disadvantage of being less specific regarding the minister's own performance, they do take into account some of the difficulties involved in performance appraisal that were outlined in Chapter 10.

In a performance appraisal that looks primarily at the program of the church, attention is drawn away from the more threatening evaluation of the clergyman himself. As a church and its pastor engage in a review of the effectiveness of its program, everyone is looking at end results. The minister receives professional feedback indirectly whenever he is able to recognize the part he has played, or failed to play, in making the program what it is. Feedback in this form may be easier to give and, for some men, easier to receive.

1. *A Congregational Self-Study.* The Lafayette-Orinda United Presbyterian Church conducted an extensive study of its program through a questionnaire distributed to 115 preselected adult members who were not members of the official boards of the church. Sixty-three responded. A second group of twenty-two adults and five young people who volunteered to fill out the questionnaire provided

a comparison group in evaluating the replies. The assumption was that the selected group was a cross-sectional sample of the congregation whereas the volunteer group would represent those who were "persons intensely interested in church affairs," including those who were "generally more voluble (and to a degree more frequently critical)." (86.) In addition to questions regarding age, marital status, length of membership, years in the community, and income level, the questionnaire asked questions such as those listed in Appendix 5.

In connection with these questions opportunity was given for respondents to state reasons for their answers. In addition, they were presented with a list of church activities. They were asked to indicate the degree of their interest in each of these activities (very interested, approve of, not interested, don't approve of).

2. *Ratings of Satisfaction and Importance.* A similar but less extensive approach to program evaluation was used by several churches in Washington, D.C. Use was made of a questionnaire that listed elements of the church program such as those shown in Appendix 6. In the "Satisfaction" column opposite each statement, church members were asked to indicate the degree of satisfaction they felt with that program element. In the "Importance" column, they were asked to indicate the degree of importance they found in each element. One church used an 11-point scale; where "0" represented "wholly dissatisfied" or "unimportant," and "10" represented "wholly satisfied" or "essential." Another church used a 5-point scale as follows:

"SATISFACTION"   (1) wholly dissatisfied;   (2) largely dissatisfied;
                 (3) mixed feelings;   (4) largely satisfied; and
                 (5) wholly satisfied.
"IMPORTANCE"   (1) unimportant;   (2) marginal;   (3) useful;
                 (4) important;   and (5) essential.

A summary of their ratings was prepared for use in a planning conference in which church officers or other members of the congregation participated. Discussion was also stimulated by a comparison of the members' answers to these questions with the minister's answers to the same questions.

3. *Time-Priority Discussions.* Another approach used by Charles

Carson in working with executives of judicatories might help a pastor improve communication with his board regarding the relation between program priorities and the way in which he spends his time.

With church executives, a series of sixty cards is used. These describe the different activities in which an executive engages, such as: attending community-related meetings, coaching and counseling staff and committees, communicating via mass media, continuing education for self and others, forecasting and planning programs, organizing the organization, preparing and delivering sermons, reading and studying, "resourcing" and motivating committees, teaching in formal situations, training church officers.

The executive is asked to sort these cards into three piles, separating those activities on which he spends *most time, least time,* and *in-between.* A counselor, meeting with him, then discusses whether or not the executive feels the time he spends is in line with his priorities and with his accountabilities. Cards may also be sorted into three other piles to indicate activities that are *most important, least important,* and *in-between.*

To facilitate a comparison of time and priority ratings, the same items might be used in a questionnaire or check list with spaces opposite each item for the respondent to indicate by check mark the relative amount of time spent on each activity and the relative importance of it. A fruitful discussion might be anticipated as a minister explores his reasons for spending more time on less important activities, or vice versa.

Where there is a multiple staff, Carson has found it helpful to ask an executive's associates to indicate their perception of how their boss spends his time. Differences between an executive's perception and that of his staff have provided the basis for valuable discussions.

The application of this process to the work of the parish minister seems obvious. The pastor could sort cards or check a form to indicate the importance he attaches to different activities and the relative amount of time he spends. A composite summary of similar opinions from members of his board could be prepared and used as the basis for a discussion that might lead to clarification of mutual expectations and the setting of goals.

One judicatory has experimented with just such a procedure in several churches as part of a pilot program entitled "Review and

Preview of the Minister's Task." The items used in their list of pastoral functions and task priorities included: reading and study, social events, community involvement, Presbytery, enlistment, counseling, visitation, scouts, camp and conferences, youth groups, adult education, released time, confirmation class, teacher training, moderating the session, worship, preaching, etc.

4. *Evaluations of Program by Church Officers.* It is, of course, possible for church officers on boards or sessions to undertake with their minister a process of their own design by which they review the various program elements, deciding how they feel about them and what ought to be done to improve them. (29.) Such a program review, if done systematically and conscientiously, is a natural way for the minister to receive helpful feedback and evaluation, particularly if he is able to participate or to lead the evaluative process with a real sense of openness and with sensitivity to subtle clues that may be given him by others who are participating in the program review. Obviously, if he is defensive about his contribution to the church's program, this will tend to reduce the number of clues that will be provided him.

5. *Mission Review for the Congregation.* One approach to program review suggests that the officers of a church select a Mission Review committee which, during the course of five or six meetings, makes an inventory of the programs being carried on by the church and its organizations, considers the implications of these activities for implicit goals that underlie them, for strengths of its local mission, and new possibilities before it. In its report to the church board, the Mission Review committee answers three basic questions:

What understanding of mission does our present program suggest?
Is our current understanding of mission adequate?
Is our program effectively related to our mission? (21:22.)

One of the principal advantages of a Mission Review process such as this is the potential depth of involvement of the congregation and its relationship in a reappraisal of their program and of the theology of mission which underlies it. Its value to the minister in appraising his ministry is likely to be in the same area. To what extent is his ministry being shaped by the program that exists in his church rather than by his goals for mission? Has he kept his own theology of mission clearly in focus, and do his activities and those of his people relate in a meaningful way to it? The answers to questions such as these can result in a very searching self-appraisal, which in turn can build a foundation for a more systematic process of goal-setting and review.

6. *Cluster Support Group Discussions.* Hawley tells of an experimental support group of ministers and church officers from ten different congregations in northwest Minnesota who have been meeting together with their wives or husbands about once a month on a Sunday afternoon and evening. By means of small-group discussion, role-playing, and other techniques they consider such subjects as: What do we like about our church? What are the strengths and weaknesses of our church? What are the greatest triumphs in which our congregation has rejoiced during the past year? What are the most serious problems facing our congregation? How do we approach problem-solving in our congregation? What are the things that we can do together as a cluster of churches that we cannot do individually? What specific programs and solutions can we attempt together to solve the serious problems facing our congregations?

While the announced purpose of these meetings is not evaluative, clearly the questions dealt with are evaluative in their implications and should provide a good deal of feedback and concrete help to sensitive pastors participating in them.

7. *Judicatory-initiated Review of Congregational Program.* There is a growing realization by judicatories that they have a responsibility to ensure some process of review in congregations at periodic intervals. If carefully conceived and administered, such programs can provide helpful opportunities for an indirect review of the clergyman's work.

A judicatory in Oregon has set up a "consultation committee" to meet with representative church officers and ministers from each congregation. (137.) These meetings will: (*a*) "take the pulse" of the congregation in relation to their concept of mission, "life style," and "potential or actual tensions or problems"; (*b*) review their records; and (*c*) discover ways in which they may "develop programs to meet congregations' needs."

In advance of meetings with congregational representatives, the consultation committee will secure from each congregation: (*a*) definitions of the mission of the local congregation prepared separately by the minister and by the church officers; (*b*) congregational records; (*c*) a copy of the annual report. These will supply data as a basis for discussion.

One church executive with considerable experience in the church believes that there should be a thorough evaluation of the life and mission of every congregation at least once every five years, done by someone from outside that local situation. The minister's evaluation would, under such a plan, be done as part of the congregational evaluation and in relation to it.

8. *Project Test Pattern*. Project Test Pattern, a pilot program conducted by The Episcopal Church, makes use of organizational development consultants to help local churches more effectively identify their own mission, organize to accomplish it, and then act on the basis of it. The goal of such advisers is to help groups "move to a more effective level of operation, at which time the advisers are no longer needed" (95:5). One of the clear by-products of the use of parish consultants has been an increased flow of information to the rector on his performance of ministry. Organizational consultants have often been able to give considerable help to clergymen in identifying changes in their style of leadership that will be more productive of their goals.

9. *Negotiating a Written Agreement*. Harry Pritchett, one of the consultants who has participated in Project Test Pattern, has developed a process for clarifying a rector's accountabilities (119). It combines evaluation of past work in the parish with the negotiation of agreed-upon expectations for future service. In a sense this method could be described in Chapter 12 under *Goal-Setting,* and may therefore serve as a transition to it.

A four-phase process leads to a written agreement on mutual expectations between the rector and his vestry. It should be initiated at least one year after the rector begins his service. Discussions take place at regular vestry meetings.

Vestry members read "The Troubles of the Clergy," which summarizes findings of the Episcopal study. Discussion, preferably as the last item on a regular vestry agenda, seeks to bring out reactions and feelings of vestry and clergy.

At a regular vestry meeting from which the rector deliberately absents himself, the senior warden leads a discussion around four questions:

What do you expect of the rector?
Is he fulfilling your expectations or not? In what ways?
What do you think the parishioners expect of the rector?
Is he fulfilling these or not? In what ways?

The senior warden makes clear that the discussion is being carried on at the rector's request and that anonymity will be kept. Following the meeting, in a face-to-face discussion, he shares with the rector a summary of the comments made at the meeting.

Prior to the next vestry meeting, all members of the vestry write down their expectations of the rector and their expectations of themselves. The rector does the same. At the meeting these are discussed openly with comments and clarification as necessary. A task force, which includes the rector, is appointed to draft a written agreement on mutual expectations.

A special vestry meeting, preferably on a Saturday morning "so that no one will feel rushed for time," considers the draft agreement and seeks "a firm contract . . . which is satisfying to all concerned."

Evaluation has prepared the way for agreement on a statement of accountabilities, or even the formulation of mutual goals.

CHAPTER 12

How Ministers and Churches
Set Goals

The preceding chapter has been concerned chiefly with the question of performance review in relation to implicit or explicit criteria such as job descriptions, accountabilities, professional standards, personal characteristics, program development, or expectations. Goal-setting, or "management by objectives," has been present in some procedures, but has not been a primary element in the methods that have been described.

This chapter brings together various approaches that concentrate more specifically upon goal-setting. Review is important insofar as it enables the minister and congregation to determine whether or not they are reaching their goals, to modify their approach in order to move more effectively toward their goals, and to set new goals for future action.

Setting Goals for the Minister

It has perhaps already been clearly enough established that the goals that a clergyman sets for himself are not necessarily identical with the goals that the congregation sets for itself. While each set of goals must be compatible, it is possible to consider them separately. The more the emphasis is placed upon the professional character of the clergyman, the more his goals can be considered apart from those of the congregation he serves. Therefore, in weighing the value of the various procedures described here, one will wish to keep clearly in mind the extent to which a particular approach provides for realistic levels of communication between the minister's goals and the goals or expectations of the congregation.

1. *PAOM: Performance Appraisal for the Ordained Ministry.* In 1967 Martin Hager, of Pampa, Texas, and five members of his congregation who were engaged in personnel management for the Cabot Corporation began intensive experimentation with management by objectives and performance appraisal as adapted to the ministry from industrial patterns. (64.) The idea, which was born in a series of business and religion seminars in the Pampa church, was tried first in that church by Mr. Hager and then further developed with five other ministers.

The distinctive features of this approach include the following:

a. An *appraiser* plays, in a modified form, the role which is usually played in industry by a supervisor. He does not have the supervisor's authority, nor does he work closely with the minister on a day-to-day basis. He is a layman chosen for his expertise in personnel management and in conducting performance appraisals.

b. There is a continuous, year-round disciplined relationship between the minister and his appraiser with monthly meetings at least for the first three months. The appraiser is "an expert in implementing ideas and goals," whose task is to listen to the minister's goals, assist him in breaking administrative problems into manageable parts, and help him relate his theology to practice, etc. He is *not* an expert on the ministry.

c. The relationship between appraiser and minister is monitored by a Performance Appraisal group of two ministers and three appraisers, who listen to tape recordings, review results of the program and make suggestions.

The process makes use of instruments adapted from those used by the Cabot Corporation, and includes several steps:

a. The basic responsibilities of the minister are clarified by an analysis of "managerial, operational and decision-making responsibilities of the job." The aim of the minister-appraiser team at this point is to "objectify" the work of the minister. In what ways does he initiate activities, or provide support to the initiatives of others? Does he have final authority in decision-making, etc.? A detailed functional study of the way the minister spends his time over a period of one month may be included in this. The end product of this phase is the preparation of a clear and concise statement of the minister's basic responsibilities in such areas as worship, Christian education, evangelism, pastoral care, stewardship, mission interpretation, staff supervision, and judicatory activities.

b. Goal-setting seeks to provide objectives that are challenging, attainable, meaningful in terms of the total task, and within the minister's control. It is urged that goals be quantitatively measurable or be stated in the form of project goals to be accomplished by a specified time. They are to be stated in terms of *results* rather than *effort* and should be relevant to the goals of congregation and higher judicatories. Some goals for personal improvement may be set, such as continuing education and improved working relationships.

c. Results of the minister's work during the past year are evaluated in terms of whether or not goals were met or exceeded. In addition to a description of actual results, the minister is asked to give his opinion of his last year's performance. Finally, he gives an overall evaluation of his total performance.

d. A rating of characteristics is prepared using the table shown in the "Performance Appraisal Guide" (Appendix 7).

e. A summary analysis of significant strengths and significant weaknesses and a place for "concluding remarks" completes the evaluation form.

2. *"Review and Preview of Work and Work Objectives."* The Performance Review program of the Presbytery of Hudson River in New York (116) has been adapted to the local church from the coaching-counseling process developed by Charles Carson for the Executive and Field Service Commission of the United Presbyterian Church. Regular "reviews and previews" of the minister's work and work objectives make use of a set of starter questions that guide him in self-evaluation as preparation for an interview with three elders of his session whom he himself has selected. What have been his objectives during the past year? His accomplishments? What resources

were needed and not available? How did the expectations of the congregation, those of the pastor, and those of the church-at-large differ from one another? What about future objectives and plans, both long and short range? (See Appendix 8.)

A representative of the ministerial relations committee of the presbytery presides at the meeting, seeking especially to facilitate interchange between the pastor and his church officers and to focus on questions that are important to the growth and development of the minister and to the effectiveness of his ministry.

The discussion begins with a consideration of task priorities (see Chapter 11). After a comparison of the task priorities as seen by pastor and elders, the group moves to a consideration of the minister's self-evaluation with shared reactions and opinions of the elders. George Beimler, chairman of the committee that conducted the pilot project, reports that most of the eighteen or so churches that have participated in this process to date have responded positively. One would suppose that the value to the minister and congregation would be proportional to the degree to which the discussion centers on a review of previously formulated goals, and on the actual formulation of clear goals for the future. The greatest benefit would likely come as the review is repeated from year to year.

In Carson's guidelines (27:2) for use of the original procedure designed for judicatory executives, he stresses the importance of developing a supportive coaching-counseling relationship centered in work objectives. Important ingredients of this approach are a climate of "trust, encouragement, appreciation, and teamwork" that clarifies the work of the pastor; stimulates thinking "rather than supplying answers or solutions"; identifies "effectiveness of performance (not personality)"; determines needs for "on-the-job development, off-the-job education, and complementary experiences"; and draws out the minister's "targets for himself and for his job." As will be stressed later, the skill of the coach-counselor is an important key to the success of this and of many other approaches outlined here.

Setting Goals for Pastor and Program

As has been pointed out, one of the difficulties with which goal-setting and review must deal is keeping a meaningful relationship between the goal-setting of the congregation and that of the pastor. Approaches outlined so far stress the latter rather than the former. This presupposes that the minister's goals will be derived from those of the congregation. Actually, if he is taking his professional responsibility seriously, the clergyman may feel that the reverse should be true. That is, he may wish to begin with his *own* goals and encourage the congregation to develop its goals in relation to those he has set for himself. An active board, on the other hand, will not be content with a passive role in the formulation of goals. The danger is that each will set goals independently of the other or that the private goals of the pastor may not coincide with the formal goals of his congregation. If role conflict is to be minimized, this should not be allowed to happen. Somehow there needs to be a dynamic interrelationship between the two goal-setting processes. Each should have a measure of independence in setting its goals, yet both should be responsive to the goals of the other and should participate in setting them.

1. *Joint Goal-Setting by Pastor and Board.* One solution to this dilemma is for the minister and his board to work jointly on the setting of goals and on reviewing progress toward them. The Presbytery of Genesee Valley has developed just such a program. (113, 114, 115.) The process of goal-setting and review was originally recommended by the committee on ministerial compensation. However, the judicatory determined that this process should be separated from consideration of renumeration.

It was then assigned to the ministerial relations committee. A major premise of the program is that the board of a church has a responsibility to lead the work of a congregation and can best do so "if it will organize its objectives into stated goals with a stated time for reaching them" (113). The guide for planning gives as examples of valid goals:

a. Revise the order of worship and include more lay participation by December 1, 1970.
b. Complete a study of Christian education materials by February 1, 1971.
c. Compile an interest finder to help plan an adult education program by August 1, 1970.

Taking the first of these goals as illustration, the guide suggests that specific responsibilities for portions of this task be identified in terms of work to be done by the minister and work to be done by committees or by others involved. For example:

a. By October 1, 1970, the worship committee will have held a consultation with a cross section of the congregation and outside experts to receive suggestions for liturgical change in our congregation.
b. By November 1, 1970, the worship committee . . . will present a preliminary order of worship for the session to study.
c. By May 31, 1970, the pastor will have written a paper on the elements, purpose and new forms of worship. He will lead the committee on worship in discussions of the paper and will serve as a resource person to the committee.

It cautions against assigning a goal to anyone without corresponding authority to reach it.

The Genesee Valley program recommends that evaluation of progress toward goals should be made at least semiannually, and in the first year of a pastorate, quarterly. A small committee is organized with two members selected by the session and two selected by the minister. This group meets with the minister periodically to evaluate the fulfillment of responsibilities by pastor and by session, giving factual statements to back up their appraisal. Having examined each goal, the committee then considers "in an overall objective manner, how well the pastor and session are doing their job."

The committee should ask: If the pastor or session has failed to complete an assignment, what factors played a part in the failure? If they accomplished an assignment in a unique and creative way, how might that be carried over into subsequent programs? How can our evaluation help the pastor and session to do a better job? Are our priorities and the delegation of authority for pursuing our goals appropriate?

The committee sets forth its findings on the "Goal-Setting and Evaluation Form" (Appendix 9) and reports directly to the session, which can thereby more effectively carry out its responsibility for leading the work of the church. Carl Smith, who helped develop this program, writes:

The major purpose of program review is to keep discussion of the pastor or staff member on the basis of his work, rather than on the basis of his personality, and to give the staff person or the pastor or the committee a more thorough understanding of their efficiency and the problems they have to solve.

2. Goal-Setting on Interrelated Parallel Tracks. Another alternative to joint planning by session and pastor is seen in the program developed by the Synod of Ohio and the Presbytery of Wooster (Ohio) for its pastors and people. (136, and 141.) It is frankly recognized that the session (hereafter called "board" in this discussion) has a responsibility for developing goals for the church and that the pastor also has a responsibility for developing goals for his ministry. In line with the philosophy of a "connectional church," the two goal-setting processes are interrelated. The presbytery (hereafter called "the judicatory") likewise develops its goals and carries certain responsibilities for guiding and providing resources for the planning and review process in the local congregation.

Figure E shows some of the many interrelationships between the church, the pastor, and the judicatory. Note particularly that the pastor participates in the formulation of the board's goals for the church, and the board reviews the pastor's "key objectives" (which will hereafter be called "key goals" in order to reserve the term "objectives" for long-range targets). As the board and the pastor develop their goals, the judicatory sets before them the planning concerns of higher judicatories. These serve as guidelines for the development of goals that are to be *their* goals. Franklin Trubee reports: "We assist them in making sure their goals are not just pious statements, but are goals that are attainable, manageable, and measurable, and are reduced to writing. Some of the first-round goals may seem very elementary, but we feel the process should be established and some success registered, after which we will nudge for goals intended to stretch the pastors, sessions, and congregations."

Board goals are submitted for approval to the congregation along with a statement of strategies by which they will be reached and the part the congregation will be expected to play in reaching them. Goals are reviewed quarterly in order to take corrective action. The annual review is more comprehensive and, in line with the typical cyclical planning process, leads to the formulation of new or revised goals. Sessions also share their goals with the national missions committee of the judicatory at the time they are formulated.

While the board engages in program planning, pastors formulate their key goals. By securing board approval of their key goals, ministers are able to have board backing in the priorities they set for

Figure E   PLACING A PASTOR IN A CHURCH IS A THREE-WAY AGREEMENT
                Adapted from Presbytery of Wooster, UPCUSA (141)

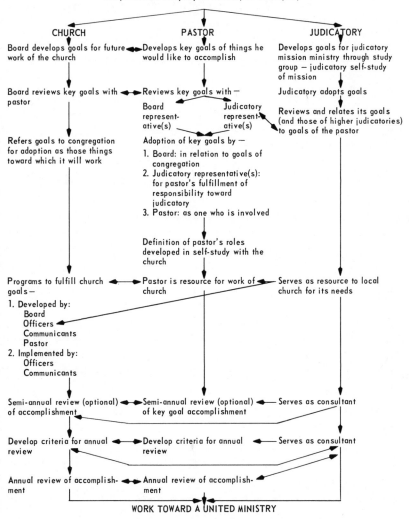

CHURCH	PASTOR	JUDICATORY

Board develops goals for future work of the church

Develops key goals of things he would like to accomplish

Develops goals for judicatory mission ministry through study group — judicatory self-study of mission

Board reviews key goals with pastor

Reviews key goals with —
Board representative(s)   Judicatory representative(s)

Judicatory adopts goals

Reviews and relates its goals (and those of higher judicatories) to goals of the pastor

Refers goals to congregation for adoption as those things toward which it will work

Adoption of key goals by —
1. Board: in relation to goals of congregation
2. Judicatory representative(s): for pastor's fulfillment of responsibility toward judicatory
3. Pastor: as one who is involved

Definition of pastor's roles developed in self-study with the church

Programs to fulfill church goals —

Pastor is resource for work of church

Serves as resource to local church for its needs

1. Developed by:
   Board
   Officers
   Communicants
   Pastor
2. Implemented by:
   Officers
   Communicants

Semi-annual review (optional) of accomplishment

Semi-annual review (optional) of key goal accomplishment

Serves as consultant

Develop criteria for annual review

Develop criteria for annual review

Serves as consultant

Annual review of accomplishment

Annual review of accomplishment

WORK TOWARD A UNITED MINISTRY

their work. In addition to board approval, pastors review their goals with the judicatory staff person who serves as the consultant in the annual evaluation.

The annual planning cycle for the pastor consists of the following steps:

1. Formulation of key goals. The source of each goal is indicated. That is, does it come from the board and its goals, from some other church organization, from the minister's own thinking, from the judicatory, etc.?

2. Discussion of key goals with the judicatory representative, who helps clarify the goals and may suggest changes.

3. Approval of key goals by board.

4. Three weeks before his annual appraisal interview, each minister evaluates his progress in realizing key goals, records his findings on the "Guide to Planned Professional Accomplishments," which includes spaces for: (a) listing the key goals; (b) sources of the goals; (c) results achieved; (d) accomplishment appraisal; (e) development plan; and (f) response to the appraisal.

Considering each objective one by one, the pastor records specific examples of accomplishment or non-accomplishment; makes appropriate quantitative and qualitative judgment, and suggests reasons for progress or lack of progress. The purpose here is for the pastor "to evaluate his own strengths, weaknesses, and potential, looking forward to improvement in skills and service." (136.)

5. Accomplishments are appraised in a personal conference between pastor and judicatory representative. They discuss accomplishments, factors relating to success, comprehensiveness and adequacy of the objectives, methods, and skills used, and ways in which the judicatory representative may be more helpful.

6. A development plan for the minister is agreed upon with the judicatory representative and recorded.

It is important to note that the self-appraisal and plans developed in the appraisal interview are not transmitted to boards. They are worked out on a professional colleague basis with the judicatory representative. Some boards, however, also conduct a review process with their pastors.

Any judicatory that plans to implement a program such as this one, which involves an intimate interchange between a pastor and an official representative of the judicatory, will wish to consider the obstacles that may need to be overcome and decide upon a stance

that will break down possible defensiveness. Franklin Trubee, minister of mission, comments on how Wooster Presbytery faced these
obstacles.

Problems in implementation involved suspicion, feeling of a heavy-
handed presbytery authority, lethargy, resistance to change. These have
been offset through responding to immediate needs, to desires for more
effective church life, to feelings of inadequacy of pastors; and have been
taken in easy steps allowing them to choose WHAT is done, by WHOM,
WHEN, and HOW, but using an orderly planning process. It is working,
and each time an elder "testifies" to achievement in presbytery the way is
made easier.

The Complex Business of Setting Goals

This is not the place to go into a lengthy discussion of the intrica-
cies of goal-setting. Those who intend to use management by objectives in their work will want to do some study and careful preparation before setting up their planning process. A book that may prove
helpful is *Managing for Results,* by Peter Drucker. Other useful
books are listed in the bibliography of this book (33, 38, 48, 89, 92,
104, 109). A few suggestions may be in order here:

1. Long-range objectives that "define the conditions to be
achieved, year after year, if the enterprise is to be successful" (104)
will help to give perspective and unity to short-range goals that are
framed each year.

2. Specific goals, which are "end results to be achieved, within
a given period of time," should concentrate on *major end results*
rather than on many different activities. A list of activities, tasks,
or projects does not qualify as a list of "goals." (104.)

3. Goals should be written in such a way that you can later
measure your progress toward reaching them. If they can be
quantitative with specific numbers or percentages, measurement
is easier. But, as has been suggested (Chapter 11), the achievement
of goals can be checked against a description of a *qualitative* condition that will prevail when the goal is reached, or against a description of some other *verifiable* condition, such as the existence

of a program, a report, a recommendation, or a decision reached.
4. Goals should be achievable, but should require stretching to reach them.

5. Measurement of progress can be further enhanced by the selection of "indicators" for each goal. "An indicator is an important factor which can be looked at, seen, or felt as a first step in determining how well a responsibility has been performed. It is evidence which can be examined and analyzed in making a judgment as to how well a job has been done." (92.) Goals may not require elaboration, in terms of indicators, if they have been written carefully as suggested in item 3, above.

6. Distinguish between *administrative goals* (which are concerned with the effective operation of a program or an institution); *sponsor benefits* (which are concerned with values that accrue to an institution as a result of a program); and *change goals* (which are specific statements regarding the way in which people, situations, or organizations will be different as the result of a program). Sometimes the real pressures behind programs may be related to the first two of these types of end result, rather than to the third, which is their formally stated purpose. Goals should deal realistically with these dimensions. If they do not, hidden conflict between them may interfere with achievement of stated goals. (104.)

7. Review progress toward goals at least quarterly, and as necessary take corrective action either to modify the goals or your plans for reaching them. The annual review will be more satisfactory if one does not wait until that time before checking on how he is doing.

How to Get Going

When a decision has been reached that something should be done about goal-setting and performance review, how does a church or judicatory go about initiating the process?

A pastor may ask his church officers to join him in a study program, which could center in the reading and discussion of a book such as this one. An even larger involvement of the congregation as a whole would be possible if this book were used by adult study groups as a basis for discussions on the subject, "What do we expect of our pastor?"

One judicatory committee, after reading an early draft of Part III of this book, planned to initiate a series of workshops on goal-setting, feedback, and performance review. Scheduled for an afternoon and evening, the workshops aimed at both pastors and lay leaders. The proposed program looked like this:

1:00 P.M. Pastors arrive, bringing a questionnaire previously mailed to them, on which they have indicated some personal expectations, aspirations, objectives, frustrations, etc.

1:00–1:30 P.M. Introductions, orientation, etc.

1:30–5:30 P.M. Workshop on the goal-setting process for pastors, joys and frustrations, sources of satisfaction, present means of performance review and evaluation, concerns and desires, etc.

4:30 P.M. Elders arrive.

4:30–5:30 P.M. Orientation of elders; workshop of "communication skills" (i.e., "how to tell what you feel").

5:30–6:30 P.M. Dinner, fellowship, introductions, etc.

6:30–9:30 P.M. (Pastors and elders together): Expression and exploration of personal and professional feelings; building the goal-setting process for the local church; implementing the process of goal-setting, feedback, and performance review in the local church.

9:30 P.M. Adjournment.

Imaginative leadership will think of many other ways to open up the subject, and it is hoped that some of the material given here will help stimulate just such leadership.

But before acting, turn to Chapter 13 and take time to consider one more vital dimension of goal-setting and review: the role of a counselor in it.

CHAPTER 13

How Counselors Facilitate
Goal-Setting and Review

Now that we have completed a survey of a rather wide variety of approaches to goal-setting and review, there is one remaining point that needs to be lifted up and underscored with considerable vigor. Whatever the forms or procedures that may be available for use by ministers, boards, or congregations, their effectiveness will depend more upon the skill and competence of those who use them than on the procedures or forms themselves, no matter how good they may be. This should be clear from the fact that industrial applications of these techniques are not uniformly successful and, further, from the complexity of applying them to the clergyman, who is—as we have shown—a professional with organizational accountability.

If this is true, it is somewhat surprising that, of the methods we have described, more do not make use of specialized help in carrying them out. Several other findings of research to which reference has already been made suggest the possibility that neutral third-party participation in the review process might considerably enhance it.

1. The "neutrality" of the discussion leader in Higgins and Dittes' experiments was thought by them to be a possible contributing factor in the reduction of role conflict through discussion.

2. Clergy do not, on the whole, appear to have accurate perceptions of the expectations of their laity, even when they work with them closely. Some mediating clarifier with professional skill might help improve communication.

3. Organizational consultants appear to have been quite effective, in Project Test Pattern experience, in dealing with communication and role problems.

The Personnel Development Interview Program

The United Presbyterian Church, the Reformed Church in America, and the Church of the Brethren have for several years been involved in a program of goal-setting and review for their missionary personnel overseas. More recently the program has been used by some personnel of the United Methodist Church, the Lutheran Church in America, and others. This author (127 and 128), working with two colleagues, Mae Ross Taylor and James Brown, developed the forms and procedures for the Personnel Development Interview program in 1967. They have now been used with well over 650 professionals (doctors, nurses, educators, and technical personnel, as well as ministers) in over thirty countries. Because overseas personnel work within widely diverse cultural and administrative contexts and under the direction of autonomous churches and institutions, the development of goal-setting and review procedures for them was an exceedingly complex process. Mission agencies in the United States, which appoint missionaries, pay the salaries, and decide whether or not they should continue in current assignments or be transferred to others, do not have the right to impose any uniform pattern upon the organizations for whom the missionaries work. Therefore, it was decided quite early in the design of these Personnel Development Interviews that a neutral third party with some skills in work-related counseling would be a necessary part of the program.

Leonard De Beer, of the Reformed Church in America, working with his colleagues in the Office of Human Resources, has adapted the Personnel Development Interview program for recommended use by parish ministers. This program combines several elements: (a) an extensive review by the minister of his own ministry, carried on with the help of a competent counselor; (b) an assessment by the congregation of its mission; (c) a process of dialogue between the pastor, church officers, and church members on the meaning and purpose of the church; and (d) the setting of goals for both pastor and congregation. The following paragraphs, adapted from the Reformed Church in America prospectus (108), summarize their approach.

The Personnel Development Interview program (PDI) offers a pastor the opportunity to assess his ministry in the light of his gifts and abilities, of his calling, and of new possibilities that God sets before him.

The PDI offers congregations the opportunity to review and evaluate the present direction and future possibilities of their church. It provides for broad participation in the setting of goals for mission. Dialogue between minister and consistory and/or [congregation] offers to both the opportunity to discuss and clarify expectations that one has of the other's role in attaining new goals for their church in its total ministry.

Before any interviews are held, the minister engages in a process of self-appraisal using a self-evaluation form [see Appendix 10], in which he reviews systematically his goals, activities, achievements, and gifts in relation to his past and possible future ministry.

At the same time, opinions on similar questions are secured on a Personnel Development Opinion survey form (PDO) [see Appendix 11] from the minister's colleagues and from several members of the consistory and congregation. The minister selects those whom he desires to fill out opinion forms. They are gathered on a confidential basis and are summarized by the counselor for his use in the interviews that follow.

Specifically, the mechanics of the interview program follow this order: a competent counselor (who comes from outside the pastor's immediate living area) spends approximately eight to ten hours with him in a series of interviews. This is Phase I of the program. The minister's wife is encouraged to participate in the interview program also.

The counselor meets with the pastor to discuss his self-evaluation and to share such information from the Opinion Survey as may be helpful to the minister's understanding of himself and his work. The effort at this point is to help him clarify and recognize his accomplishments, consider related personal and family matters, and explore areas for future growth.

In the case of a couple, the counselor first meets alone with the husband, then with the wife. Finally he meets with the couple together. This gives opportunity for each person to talk with the counselor about professional, personal, or marital concerns that can most easily be raised in a one-to-one setting. What are their attitudes and feelings about their present life situation? Does the pastor find his present work fulfilling and worthwhile as a part of his calling? What are the problems of his personal work involvement? The helping process consists of enabling the person to ask some hard questions about where he is in the present situation, questions such as:

Is this where I want to be? (How is my role affecting me and my family today?)

What in actuality is my task, and do I find it fulfilling?

What are my attitudes toward the ministry?

What are my goals?

Are my goals reachable, realistic, constructive?

What are the possible paths to these goals?

Which is the most direct path?

It is in this beginning Phase I that the counselor seeks to understand the minister as a *person* and as a *professional,* attempting to sort out *personal and family* concerns and *vocational* ones. . . . Clarification to some degree results when the minister sees that he is being heard and understood and is able to share his life situation with the counselor in a trust relationship. Clarification also takes place as he receives feedback as to how his colleagues and others with whom he works perceive him.

Phase II of the program involves the participation of the consistory as well as the pastor and counselor. Normally, such gatherings are held within the week after Phase I. There is no exact time sequence to be followed.

What is the purpose of Phase II? It is hoped that the first phase has enabled the minister to see things more clearly in relation to his life situation and calling. New possibilities and options in regard to future ministry may have surfaced along with clarification of the issues that have frustrated him. Together with the consistory, he now has the opportunity to share and explore mutual expectations as to their roles, differences of outlook, dreams for the future—the stuff from which goals are made. The counselor acts as a facilitator, assisting both pastor and consistory to hear and to understand each other, thus laying the groundwork for congregational planning and goal-setting. Phase II may be an evening meeting or a day retreat with pastor and consistory determining time and place.

Phase III has as its purpose the participation and involvement of the total church leadership and membership-at-large in the goal-setting process. [See Appendix 12.] A weekend workshop together may be most productive in creating future goals.

The counselor in Phase III takes on more of a consultant's role, facilitating communication whenever necessary, but remaining somewhat in the background. Preceding work with elected church leaders in Phases I and II should enable them to exert leadership in the workshop. Indeed, this is most desirable. However, the counselor/consultant may take a more aggressive role at times in discussing action-planning, implementation, and evaluation in the planning process.

Is the Program Valuable?

Since the Reformed Church in America has just initiated the use of the Personnel Development Interview program with its pastors, it is too early to have any evaluation of its effectiveness for the parish ministry. With the overseas program, however, there has been a continual feedback evaluation process from the beginning. Each participant is asked to fill out an anonymous evaluation form at the conclusion of his series of interviews. When asked to indicate the value of the experience in terms of its helpfulness to them, 210 people (57 percent of the 368 replies that have been tabulated) indicated that the Personnel Development Interviews were either "extremely helpful" or "very helpful" to them. If one includes those who felt they were "fairly helpful," the percentage of respondents rises to 80 percent (293 people). When one considers that, for most of the respondents, participation in the program was mandatory, this indicates a rather positive response.

Although no control group exists that could test the relative value of trying to accomplish the same results without the use of "neutral" counselors from outside the working context of the participants, it is clear to those who have been directing the program that without such counselors (the distinctive feature), *nothing at all* would have been possible.

It's the Counselor Who Counts

The critical importance of the competence of the counselor seems to emerge from a tabulation of the evaluation forms by country of residence and by counselors. Of the counselors who conducted more than ten interviews, one had 80 percent who rated their experience with him as either "extremely helpful" or "very helpful." In contrast, another counselor had *no* such ratings in those categories. If one compares the work of different counselors working in the same country, it seems clear that those who have been effective in one country tend to be effective in other countries. Whereas contextual factors do affect the process, they do not appear to have been as determinative in the outcome as the skill of the counselor.

Our findings, then, reinforce what was said at the beginning of this chapter. Whatever forms or procedures may be available for use by ministers, boards, or congregations, their effectiveness will depend more upon the skill and competence of those who use them than on the procedures and forms themselves, no matter how good these may be.

This also strongly suggests that for goal-setting and review, more experimentation should be carried on in the use within parish contexts of neutral third-party counselors and consultants. This is one of the advantages of the new Reformed Church in America Personnel Development Interview process. It makes use of trained counselors who are not directly or personally involved either in the dynamics of the local parish or in the politics of the judicatory to which the minister belongs.

CHAPTER 14

Putting It All Together

We have now surveyed a rather broad range of experiments in the use of goal-setting and performance review. What generalizations and suggestions emerge that may guide further efforts in this area? What elements should be brought into procedures so that both pastor and people can be helped to work together more effectively in relation to clear goals?

1. *Clarify your mission.* At the beginning of a pastoral relationship, it is important to be clear on what the mission of the church is. Not everyone will agree, but even before a minister is called the people should come to some consensus on what the church is all about and why they are in business as a congregation. The prospective pastor should know the overarching purpose of the congregation he is to serve. If the pastor and congregation do not agree on their purpose, there will be stress in the relationship.

2. *Define your accountabilities.* This is, of course, another way of saying that the minister and his board need to think through what each of them expects of the other. In what way is the minister expected to contribute toward the purpose of the church? What end results is he responsible to bring about? What, in turn, can he expect of his board and of the congregation?

3. *Set up a cyclical planning process.* Set long-range objectives and short-range goals. The board should lead the congregation in developing goals that will contribute to your purpose as a church. As goals are established, consider how you will measure the attainment of each goal. Check progress toward your goals frequently and take corrective action. At least once a year, review carefully the work

you have been doing, and determine whether or not you have reached your goals. Set new goals and revise those which continue to be relevant as a basis for the new year's work.

4. *Relate the goals of the pastor to the goals of the people.* As a professional, the minister should have goals that are uniquely his own. They need to be relevant to and contribute toward the goals of the congregation. His board should share in their formulation at least to the extent of reviewing them and of agreeing that they are both appropriate and consistent with the purpose and program of the church. He should include goals for professional and personal development.

5. *Evaluation of program and appraisal of staff performance are intimately interrelated.* In a consideration of the effectiveness of a minister, the focus should be on end results rather than on personal characteristics. As pastor and people together set goals and measure their accomplishment, they have a concrete basis for weighing the effectiveness of the pastoral relationship.

6. *Self-evaluation is an essential ingredient in an appraisal process.* Some form of guide for the minister to use in evaluating his ministry will help him to do so systematically.

7. *Some method of gathering data in addition to the self-evaluation is useful.* Preferably such material should be summarized so as to ensure the anonymity of those who have provided it. It should then be shared with the minister and discussed in connection with the minister's self-evaluation.

8. *A visiting counselor or consultant can make an important contribution to the review process.* A counselor may be especially helpful if he is not administratively responsible for the employment of the minister, and if he has special competence to help the minister clarify his goals, look objectively at his ministry, understand his strengths and weaknesses, and set realistic goals for his development. There should be a time in the process when the consultant meets alone with the minister in relation to his self-evaluation. There may be problems in his ministry that he feels he cannot share with his board or with members of his congregation. He should have opportunity to reflect on these with someone. He may have personal or family problems that affect his work and that need to be worked through. He needs to establish clear long-range vocational and per-

sonal goals that do not necessarily relate directly to the goals of the congregation he is serving.

9. *The local church board needs to participate meaningfully in the review process.* For a review to be carried on without their involvement is to risk widening any gaps that may exist between them and their minister. If a visiting counselor is used in the process, he becomes a process consultant when working with the board and congregation.

10. *A personnel committee of the church board may prove to be helpful in working with the minister and other staff members in defining their responsibilities and in carrying out regular performance reviews.* Such a committee should probably not have more than five members, who should be selected for their skill in working with people and preferably for their professional expertise in the personnel field.

11. *A performance review that is not linked with salary review appears to have the potential of being more helpful to the staff participant.*

12. *In view of the important role that the clergyman's wife plays in his vocational decisions, more attention needs to be given to ways in which she may be meaningfully involved in the setting of goals and in their review.* A time may well be set aside by a counselor to meet with her alone and with her husband. Depending on how she views her role in the church, she herself may wish to set goals and engage in some form of self-evaluation. In any case, the lack of participation of the minister's wife in most of the programs that have been described here would appear to be an important factor for further study.

Where Do We Go from Here?

As has been clear throughout this study, the church is just on the threshold of understanding some of the dynamics of the clergyman's role conflicts and ambiguities. There have been some tentative moves in the direction of finding solutions. A good deal of concern about the issues involved is evident throughout the church. That in itself is a healthy sign and an important first step toward minimizing the problems. Much openness and creative experimentation is required if further progress is to be made. Perhaps some of the clues that have been provided here will help to stimulate the opening of new doors to the future.

APPENDIXES

PERFORMANCE RATING LEVELS
PRESBYTERY OF MONMOUTH, UPCUSA (149)

A. OUTSTANDING

This term applies to those individuals who in a given characteristic consistently and without question exceed all normal expectations of performance.

B. EXCELLENT

This rating applies to those who meet or exceed the major requirements of the job in a given characteristic, covering a broad range of performance of completely acceptable work.

C. AVERAGE

This rating applies to those who do what is expected and required but no more in a given characteristic. Sometimes their work reaches the lower limit of acceptability, although they may reach a level approaching Excellent in varying degrees occasionally, but with no consistency. They sometimes show deficiencies that prevent them from performing in a completely acceptable manner.

D. UNSATISFACTORY

This rating covers individuals who do not have either the capability or the determination to carry out job responsibilities as assigned in a given characteristic. It includes those who have failed to improve performance to an acceptable extent after a previous performance review, or after some constructive effort has been made to counsel them about such improvement.

E. UPPER AND LOWER HALF

It will be noted that each block . . . [has] two dotted lines so that it is therefore subdivided into three parts. This is so that those who wish to distinguish degrees of performance within a particular range may do so.

COMPETENCE IN THE PARISH MINISTRY
A statement adopted by the Academy of Parish Clergy, Inc., for testing and study (2)

RECOMMENDATIONS of the Committee on Standards of Competence:
  1. That the Academy adopt the following statement of Areas of Competence for a period of one year.
  2. That the Board of Directors establish a permanent Committee on Standards of Competence and keep this before the Academy for purposes of review and revision.
  3. That individual members be urged to evaluate their practice according to these standards.

STATEMENT OF OVERALL PURPOSE OF THE PARISH MINISTRY:
  To enable persons to create caring community that brings them to a full realization of their humanity.

RECOGNIZING THAT each parish is understood in terms of its social, economic, political, cultural, and geographical context, ministerial skills are matched to different situations. A parish clergyman develops skills that are useful in his unique situation. The practice of parish ministry includes the following areas:

I. COMMUNICATION SKILLS

A. Spoken, written, and nonverbal communication skills, with capacity to express and perceive in a broad range.

B. Ability to interpret symbols of the past, present, and future, and to show their relevance (e.g., the Bible).

C. Skill in helping others to communicate, including the use of all media.

II. RELATION-BUILDING SKILLS
Skills enabling self and others to form enduring and effective connections —

A. Between person and self (soul) (e.g., convictions, values).

B. Between person and God (e.g., prayer, meditation, healing, spirituality).

C. Between person and person (e.g., social, friendships, counseling, confrontation, family life).

D. Between person and congregation (e.g., recreation, amusement, task groups).

E. Between congregation and community (e.g., community service, higher church politics, challenge to society).

III. PARTICIPATORY MANAGEMENT SKILLS
(Skills appropriate to voluntary organizations)

A. Legislative (major policy-making) (e.g., chairmanship and mediator skills, change agent techniques, creative utilization of conflict).

B. Administrative (organization and coordination)
  1. Fund-raising and allocation.
  2. Use and care of facilities.
  3. Recruitment of leaders and new participants.

C. Evaluative
  1. Planning process.
  2. Review procedure.
  3. Institutionalization of change (procedures for self-renewal).

IV. LEARNING SKILLS
(Skills leading to growth in competence)

A. Ability to analyze the congregation and situation.

B. Referral and use of outside resources.

C. Clarification of clergy and congregation's mutual expectations.

D. Facility in teaching history and principle, using all methods: experiential, multimedia, and didactic.

E. Case study (reflection) on clergyman's own work, with standards for self-evaluation and opportunity for continuous feedback.

F. Use of continuing education and career development opportunities.

G. Utilization of consultative and professional help on the scene.

H. Consultative skills, including leadership and team-training skills.

V. CELEBRATION-WORSHIP SKILLS

A. Preaching and response-gathering.

B. Familiarity with traditional, contemporary, and emerging forms of worship, including all media of expression.

C. Mobilizing creativity of groups (especially worship-planning groups), enabling self-expression and spontaneity.

GUIDELINES FOR USING THE PASTORAL PERFORMANCE RECORD
Presbytery of Indianapolis, UPCUSA (117)

The following questions are intended as guides in the use of the "Pastoral Performance Record." They are suggestive of what might be considered in the evaluation of each activity.

ADMINISTRATION
Does he get maximum performance from members of the staff? Does he delegate authority well? Are goals clearly defined and communicated? Are deadlines established and adhered to?

CHURCH EDUCATION
Does he evidence interest in and support of this program? Is he aware of the problems and new trends? Does he understand the scope to include more than the Sunday church school? Does he have program ideas?

CHURCH FINANCE
Is he aware of the church's financial situation? Do areas for which he is responsible stay within budget? Are adequate records kept? Is there a year-round program to develop financial support?

COMMUNITY ACTIVITIES
Is he known within the community? Does he take a reasonably active part in community affairs? Does he represent the church well to the community? Does he evidence concern for the community?

CONTINUED EDUCATION
Does he take advantage of study opportunities? Does he evidence growth from these opportunities?

COUNSELING
Is he available? Does he respect confidences? Is there premarital and prebaptismal counseling? Has he attended conferences or institutes on the subject?

EVANGELISM
Is there a session committee? Is there a planned program of visitation on newcomers and the unchurched? Do sermons reflect the "good news"? How many adult baptisms were there last year?

GENERAL ATTITUDE
Is he genuinely interested in people? Does he reflect real enthusiasm? Does he have a positive attitude?

PASTORAL CALLING
Does he have a planned program? Are calls made on significant occasions, i.e., birth, baptism, confirmation, marriage, sickness, death? Do his calls have a point (avoid the numbers game)?

PREACHING
Do his sermons reflect study? Are they well organized? Is there variety in his preaching? Are the topics timely and relevant? (Do *not* evaluate on the basis of *agreement* or *disagreement!*)

PRESBYTERY AND SYNOD RESPONSIBILITIES
Is he faithful in his attendance? Are the session and congregation kept informed of major actions of the other judicatories?

RELATIONSHIPS
Does he have the confidence of the staff, leaders, and congregation? Are his working relationships harmonious? Is disagreement a cause for growth or turmoil?

TEACHING

Is he well prepared? Does he utilize various teaching techniques? Does he stimulate discussion and questions? Does he keep the class on the track?

WORK WITH COMMITTEES

Does he give overall guidance as to the committee's function? Does he provide proposals and suggestions as starters? Does he follow through in implementing decisions made? Are decisions made by the committee?

WRITING

Does not imply "publish or perish," but credit should be given for published articles.

Appendix 4

SAMPLE FORMAT FOR RECORDING PERFORMANCE STANDARDS AND RELATED RATINGS (20:27)

Job Segments and Performance Standards	Time Schedule	Performance Based on Agreed-upon Standards (Check the appropriate level of performance.)				(Describe results and why they are above or below standard.)
		Well Above Std.	Above Std.	Meets Std.	Below Std.	
Job Segment: Performance Standard. Performance is up to standard when:						
1.						
2.						
3. (etc.)						

PERFORMANCE ANALYSIS

HIGH ACHIEVEMENT AREAS
(In what parts of the job does the minister excel?)

IMPROVED RESULTS POSSIBLE
(Where are improvements needed?)

1.

2.

3. (etc.)

1.

2.

3.

IMPROVEMENT PLAN

ACTION TO BE TAKEN   WHEN?   BY WHOM?

1.

2.

3. (etc.)

SOME QUESTIONS USED IN CONGREGATIONAL QUESTIONNAIRE
Lafayette-Orinda United Presbyterian Church (86)

What were your reasons for joining the church?

Has this church fulfilled your reason(s) for joining or attending?

In what ways have you been disappointed?

Do you feel you are kept adequately informed about church affairs?
_____Yes   _____ Partially   _____No

What do you feel are the church's primary responsibilities to its members?

How well do you believe this church is meeting these responsibilities?
_____Very well   _____ Adequately   _____ Inadequately

What do you believe are the church's primary responsibilities (if any) to the community-at-large?

How well do you believe the church is meeting these responsibilities?
_____Very well   _____Adequately   _____Inadequately

Do you believe that your replies (as to the church's responsibilities) are different than they might
have been when you first joined this church or began attending?
_____Yes   _____ No

What do you feel is most satisfying in your present relationship with this church?

What do you feel is least satisfying in your present relationship with this church?

How would you describe this church to a new resident of the community? [This question seemed to
provide helpful answers.]

What is your preferred time for worship services?   _____ 8 A.M., _____9:30 A.M., _____11 A.M.,
_____ Other

How often do you attend Sunday worship services?   _____ Almost every week, _____at least twice a
month, _____about once a month, _____less than once a month.

What subject matter do you prefer to see covered in sermons?

Do you have any suggestions for making worship services more meaningful to you?

Do you feel our church school and young people's programs are adequate?

What changes in emphasis (if any) would you like to see made at this church?

If you have any other concerns about your Christian commitment or fellowship, won't you relate them
here?

SAMPLE QUESTIONS FOR SATISFACTION-IMPORTANCE EVALUATION
Adapted from Charles E. Carson

(On this questionnaire, each program element is listed in a question beginning with the words, "Are you satisfied — ?" Rating may range in degree from 1 to 5, or from 0 to 10.)

SATISFACTION   IMPORTANCE

I. WORSHIP AND CHURCH LIFE
with the Sunday morning worship service? _____ _____
with the music and choir program? _____ _____
with the content of the sermons? _____ _____
with the delivery of the sermons? _____ _____
with the ushering? _____ _____
with the role that prayer plays in our church? _____ _____

II. ORGANIZATION AND ADMINISTRATION
with congregational participation in church decisions? _____ _____
that the session does enough long-range planning? _____ _____
with the newsletter? _____ _____
with the physical care and cleanliness of the church buildings? _____ _____
that you receive adequate information about church finances? _____ _____

III. EVANGELISM — CHURCH AND SOCIETY — MISSION EDUCATION
that session members attempt to call on all church members yearly? _____ _____
with the amount of pastoral calling done? _____ _____
that the church is providing Christian leadership in the community? _____ _____

IV. CHRISTIAN EDUCATION
with the quality of church school teaching? _____ _____
that the church school teacher receives adequate training? _____ _____
with the program of the Junior High Fellowship? _____ _____

V. CHRISTIAN TRAINING — STEWARDSHIP
with the amount of benevolence giving? _____ _____
with the effectiveness of the Every Member Canvass? _____ _____
with the effort made to involve all new members in the life of the church? _____ _____

PERFORMANCE APPRAISAL GUIDE FOR THE PARISH MINISTRY — WORK SHEET (58)

Name_____ Church _____
                                            Name   City

General Assembly Statistic Report for past year: Session standing committees
    Total communicants   _____   _____
    Total gains   _____   _____
    Total losses   _____   _____
    Church school membership   _____   _____
    Current receipts   _____   _____
    Special receipts   _____   Diaconate standing committees
    Benevolences   _____   _____
    Presbytery and synod   _____   _____
    General Assembly reports   _____   _____
                                _____   _____
    TOTAL   _____   _____

If the church publishes a church directory containing essential congregational information, please attach to form.
    Appraiser_____ Dates of interviews _____

A. Basic responsibilities within the context of congregational and presbytery duties.

    Congregational: Presbytery:

B. Goals for the coming year (state succinctly and realistically).
   (List goals from 1 to 11).

C. Results during the past year.
   Part 1. Actual results of goals set for self:

   Part 2. Opinion of last year's performance:

   Overall individual progress: Attained expectation_____ Exceeded_____ Fell short_____

D. Overall evaluation of total performance (circle most applicable number, from 6, highest performance, to 1, poorest performance).

6	5	4	3	2	1
Above Average Range		Average Range		Below Average Range	

E. Rating of Characteristics

Characteristics	Strongest (Check one)	Above Average (Check three)	Average (Check six)	Below Average (Check three)	Weakest (Check one)
1. Leadership					
2. Planning & organizing ability					
3. Analytical ability					
4. Judgment					
5. Work capacity					
6. Reliability					
7. Creativeness					
8. Adaptability to change					
9. Communication ability					
10. Vocation consciousness					
11. Empathy					
12. Development of lay leadership					
13. Ability to appraise people					
14. Motivation and initiative					

F. What are your significant strengths?
G. What are your most significant weaknesses?
H. Concluding remarks:

APPENDIXES

PASTOR'S SELF-EVALUATION
Presbytery of Hudson River (116)

The purpose of the evaluation and the review is to strengthen supportive relationships and to increase the effectiveness of cooperative ministry in the congregation.

Starter Questions. These questions are designed for the guidance of the person who is evaluating his own work. They are to be used for "homework" before the interview by the pastor and two elders.

I. Regarding the last twelve months:
   A. What were your very specific work objectives (goals)?
   B. How well do you think you accomplished them?
   C. Illustrate with two or three examples of what you did, or what part you played in achieving these objectives.
   D. What other resources did you need that you did not have or use?

II. Regarding the definition of your work:
   A. What does the congregation expect of you as a pastor?
   B. Do you see important points of difference with your expectations of yourself?
   C. What does the church-at-large (presbytery, synod, General Assembly) expect of you? Does that conflict with your own expectations?

III. Regarding the next twelve months and beyond:
   A. What are your specific work objectives for the next year?
   B. How do you see yourself achieving these objectives?
   C. What long-range objectives do you have for yourself and the parish you serve?
   D. What specifically will have to be done to achieve them?

IV. A. If you had the power and the resources available, what are some actions or recommendations you would pursue?
   B. If your constituency were listening, what would you like to say to them about yourself, their job, your work, and the church's mission?
   C. If you have additional reflections, feel free to express them.

What will be the point of tension or difference with the church in regard to these objectives?

What specific steps can you take to foster constructive communication at these points of difference

GOAL-SETTING AND EVALUATION FORM FOR THE WORK OF SESSIONS AND PASTORS
Presbytery of Genesee Valley (115)

Year_____
Interim review or revision of these goals to be made:_____;_____;_____.

GOALS AND RESPONSIBILITY. (All goals should be specific and within the authority of the person(s) assigned.)	Completion Date	EVALUATION. Categorize as success or failure, and give reasons.
Worship		
Christian education		
Community outreach		
Stewardship		
Pastoral care		

NOTE: These are only *suggested* areas where goals might be set. The goals of a particular church should be related to that church's mission.

208

PERSONNEL DEVELOPMENT PROGRAM
SELF-EVALUATION WORK SHEET (108)

The following questions have been designed to help you evaluate professional, personal, and family factors related to your ministry. This self-evaluation should make a valuable contribution to your planning and professional growth, by helping you evaluate your present and future goals, personal and professional. It is designed to analyze your strengths and weaknesses and to assist you in changing what you feel needs to be changed without too much confusion and discomfort in looking to the future.

Setting goals and evaluating ourselves is hard work. However, given serious thought, this self-evaluation will help you and your Personnel Development Counselor prepare for your interviews. It is confidential; it will be returned to you at the close of your discussions with your counselor.

If the space provided for any question is too small, please continue your answer on another sheet.

Name: _____   Date: _____

1. My specific work responsibility. (Wives should include their activities and work responsibilities.) What have been the aims, goals, or end results that have been set for me in my present responsibilities?	Completely 1	Almost Completely 2	Considerably 3	Somewhat 4	Hardly at All 5	Not at All 6	COMMENTS
To what extent has each goal been achieved?							

2. What are the activities connected with my present work and ministry, such as counseling, preaching, community action concerns, etc.? (Don't forget to list the routine duties often overlooked. Wives should include activities outside the home as well as those in the home and estimate the relative amount of time spent in each.)	To what extent has each activity contributed to reaching goals?					
	Completely 1	Almost Completely 2	Considerably 3	Somewhat 4	Hardly at All 5	Not at All 6

3. Which of the activities listed in the preceding item have I found the most satisfying? Which have given me a sense of achievement? (List the three most important. Define the satisfying factors in these activities if possible.)

4. What have been the principal frustrations or obstacles in my present place of service and living situation? (Wives should include family circumstances.)

5. Of the obstacles or frustrations listed in the preceding item, which stands out as the most important?

   Which affects your life where you are most concerned?

   Is it a problem in which you are personally involved? (Problems in the abstract add to the confusion, so *be specific*.)

   Realistically, do you have possibilities for influencing the situation?

   Define and describe the problem.

6. How has my picture of my work changed with experience? To what extent have I been able to create or discover in it dimensions not originally conceived?

7. What sense of vocation ("calling") do I have in my work, and how does it compare with my early sense of vocation?

8. The degree to which I feel I possess the quality described in each phrase below is indicated by the rating checked in the appropriate column opposite it.

QUALITIES	Not Applicable	Outstanding 1	Very Good 2	Good 3	Satisfactory 4	Fair 5	Poor 6	EXAMPLES
A. PROFESSION AND WORK								
1. Using professional competence								
2. Growing professionally								
3. Carrying out my responsibilities								
4. Initiating appropriate activities without being asked								

QUALITIES	Not Applicable	Outstanding 1	Very Good 2	Good 3	Satisfactory 4	Fair 5	Poor 6	EXAMPLES
5. Setting work priorities and keeping them								
6. Suggesting creative ideas								
7. Accepting ideas of others								
B. TEAMWORK								
1. Providing leadership when needed								
2. Following other leaders helpfully								
3. Releasing responsibility when I should								
4. Encouraging leadership								
C. RELATIONSHIPS								
1. Relating well to most people								
2. Quickly sensing how others feel								
3. Expressing my positions clearly								
4. Expressing my positions diplomatically								
5. Listening to others, whether or not I agree with them								
6. Being a peacemaker or reconciler								
D. PERSONALITY								
1. Usually being cheerful; seldom being depressed								
2. Persevering against obstacles								
3. Controlling my temper								
4. Being constructive and helpful in my criticism of others								
5. Maintaining poise in embarrassing situations								

QUALITIES	Not Applicable	Outstanding 1	Very Good 2	Good 3	Satisfactory 4	Fair 5	Poor 6	EXAMPLES
6. Being free from anxiety or nervousness								
7. Accepting criticism graciously								
8. Accepting praise graciously								
E. FAMILY								
1. Being supportive and encouraging of husband or wife								
2. Having a happy Christian home								
3. Children being happy and creative								

9. What are my strong points personally and professionally as I perceive myself?

10. What are my weak points personally and professionally as I perceive myself?

11. What difficulties have I had in human relations with colleagues, consistory members, members of my church?

12. How have I dealt with them?

13. To what extent do my present responsibilities make use of my abilities, interests, training, and experience? (Be specific as to which are not now being adequately used.)

14. In the light of my achievements, strengths, and limitations, what would an ideal job be like?

15. What alternative types or places of work might I consider, if I did not continue where I am now?

16. To what extent have I been growing personally, professionally, and spiritually?

17. What resources have I been able to use that have contributed to growth?

18. What reading has influenced my thinking most in the past two years?

19. How do I assess the current state of my physical health in relation to present and future demands of my work? What health checkups are indicated at this time?

20. How do I assess the current state of my emotional health and well-being? What checkups in this area might be helpful at this time?

21. How do I feel about trends and policies of the denomination, local judicatory, institution, or church where I serve?

PERSONNEL DEVELOPMENT PROGRAM
PERSONNEL DEVELOPMENT OPINION SURVEY (108)
"Having gifts that differ . . . let us use them." — Rom. 12:6

(Please do *not* put your name anywhere on this survey.)

The person named below is participating in Personnel Development Interviews to help him plan for growing effectiveness in his work, and to insure his service in work for which he is best suited. He will engage in an extensive self-evaluation, which the Personnel Development Counselor will then compare with a summary of evaluations by others.

Will you please help by filling out this Personnel Development Opinion survey?

Your opinions will not be shown to the person being interviewed. Please keep your reply in confidence.

Your opinions will be combined with the opinions of others to form a total picture of how others view this person and his work. No single opinion will be given importance except as it is confirmed by the opinions of others. Therefore, do not hesitate to give your opinion, even if you are a little uncertain about it.

After reading all the questions, please go through as quickly as possible, giving your answers to the easy questions and leaving others blank. Then go back to finish the difficult questions. Finally, place a question mark by questions on which you feel you have little or no basis for opinion.

Thank you for your help.

....

Name of participant_____　Date _____

How well do you know him?	How long have you known him?
( ) Intimately ( ) Very Well ( ) Fairly Well ( ) Casually	_____ years

Do you work directly with him? ( ) Yes ( ) No	In what capacity?
	( ) Friend ( ) Fellow worker ( ) Other

Through what other means do you know him?

1. Please read each phrase quickly and place a check mark opposite it in the column that best indicates the extent to which you feel the person named above has the quality or ability described.

QUALITIES	Not Applicable	Outstanding 1	Very Good 2	Good 3	Satisfactory 4	Fair 5	Poor 6	EXAMPLES
A. PROFESSION AND WORK								
1. Using professional competence								
2. Growing professionally								
3. Carrying out responsibilities								
4. Initiating appropriate activities without being asked								
5. Setting work priorities and keeping them								

QUALITIES	Not Applicable	Outstanding 1	Very Good 2	Good 3	Satisfactory 4	Fair 5	Poor 6	EXAMPLES
6. Suggesting creative ideas								
7. Accepting ideas of others								
B. TEAMWORK 1. Providing leadership when needed								
2. Following other leaders helpfully								
3. Releasing responsibility when appropriate								
4. Encouraging leadership								
C. RELATIONSHIPS 1. Relating well to most people								
2. Quickly sensing how others feel								
3. Expressing positions clearly								
4. Expressing positions diplomatically								
5. Listening to others, whether or not in agreement								
6. Being a peacemaker or reconciler								
D. PERSONALITY 1. Usually being cheerful; seldom being depressed								
2. Persevering against obstacles								
3. Controlling temper								
4. Being constructive and helpful in criticism of others								
5. Maintaining poise in embarrassing situations								
6. Being free from anxiety or nervousness								
7. Accepting criticism graciously								
8. Accepting praise graciously								
E. FAMILY 1. Being supportive and encouraging of husband or wife								
2. Having a happy Christian home								
3. Children being happy and creative								

2. Please list this person's major accomplishments during the past few years, including creative contributions to the work and the life of the church.

3. Please check below in the appropriate column the words or phrases which, in your opinion, describe the strengths, also the greatest strengths, of this person. Since no person is without limitations of some kind, also place a check in the column headed "limitations" before the words or phrases that represent qualities which, in your opinion, need to be developed in this person.

Greatest Strengths	Strengths	Limitations		Greatest Strengths	Strengths	Limitations	
___	___	___	adaptability	___	___	___	well-meaning
___	___	___	administrative ability	___	___	___	leadership ability
___	___	___	attractive personality	___	___	___	listening ability
___	___	___	good judgment	___	___	___	maturity
___	___	___	calmness	___	___	___	optimism
___	___	___	clear thinking	___	___	___	patience
___	___	___	commitment to Christ	___	___	___	perseverance
___	___	___	compassion	___	___	___	professional ability
___	___	___	courage	___	___	___	resourcefulness
___	___	___	counseling ability	___	___	___	self-confidence
___	___	___	creativity	___	___	___	appreciativeness
___	___	___	communication ability	___	___	___	sense of humor
___	___	___	dependability	___	___	___	service motivation
___	___	___	emotional stability	___	___	___	small-group leadership
___	___	___	energy	___	___	___	spiritual depth
___	___	___	enthusiasm	___	___	___	tact
___	___	___	foresight	___	___	___	teaching ability
___	___	___	levelheadedness	___	___	___	thoroughness
___	___	___	friendliness	___	___	___	thoughtfulness
___	___	___	hard work	___	___	___	tolerance
___	___	___	honesty	___	___	___	understanding of people
___	___	___	humility	___	___	___	steady nerves
___	___	___	_____	___	___	___	_____

4. Please check the appropriate box after each question.

	Emphatically Yes	Yes	Maybe	Probably Not	No
A. Would you like to work with this person as your supervisor?					
B. Would you like to work with him as your colleague?					
C. Would you like to work with him as your assistant?					

D. What is your reason for the answers you have given?

5. If you know of an incident where you wanted to explain this person's actions to someone else, felt some embarrassment on his behalf, or wanted to apologize for him, please describe it.

6. Please check the phrase that best describes this person's physical health:

             (   ) Poor   (   ) Good

             (   ) Relatively poor   (   ) Excellent

             (   ) Fair

Please comment:

7. Please evaluate this person's emotional health and estimate what effect it may have on his future service.

8. What future study, experience, observation, counseling, or other development would you suggest for this person?

CHURCH DEVELOPMENT PROGRAM
CHURCH GOAL-SETTING WORK SHEET (108)
"Having gifts that differ . . . let us use them." — Rom. 12:6

If you have taken seriously the task of filling out the Church Profile form, you now have some idea as to "what" your congregation has been about in recent years doing "kingdom" work. You may also have some ideas as to the direction you think the church should take in mission work in future years, what your pastor's role should be, and what your role and task may be.

Use this paper to do "thinking" in writing. List some of the goals you see for your congregation. In doing so, be as specific as possible. Dealing with the abstract adds to confusion.

1. What goals would you set for your congregation in its mission during the next few years?

2. Of the list of goals in question 1, *which two* would you say are the most important? Here are suggestions for selecting the goals: (a) They are concerns that you feel would enhance and further the life and ministry of your church. (b) They are goals that concern you, and that are reachable by prayer and hard work.

3. Most goal statements can be rephrased so that they describe two things: (a) the situation as it is now, and (b) the situation as you think it should be ideally.

   Restate the two goals listed above, indicating the direction of the change you desire. Examples: (poor) "We can't hold on to our youth because . . . " and (better), "We should develop programs that will meet the needs of our young people."

4. How do these goals relate to what your pastor does timewise in his ministry? What two areas of activity should be given major emphasis in his division of time?

5. What specific *skills* and general *aptitude* do you feel is needed in your pastor to best meet the above-mentioned needs and goal areas? (E.g., "We need a dedicated man to call on community newcomers.")

(The following three questions are to be answered by the pastor.)

6. What resources are available among the members of your congregation for achieving the church's mission goals? Think in terms of possibilities. Are there resource people not being used?

7. What are the goals I want to set for myself as a person in the larger context of the life and mission of the church — in relation to the goals listed in question 1?

8. In what areas do I feel the most need for growth? (What knowledge, skills, attitudes do I want to acquire?)

CONSULTANTS

The following persons were consulted, either in person or by correspondence. They served in many different ways: as sources of materials or as sources of important ideas or perspectives. Some read and commented on the manuscript. Their help is gratefully acknowledged. (NOTE: the abbreviation UPCUSA is used to refer to The United Presbyterian Church in the U.S.A.)

Adams, Henry B., Executive Director, Academy of Parish Clergy.
Baker, Blaine, Director, Management Development Institute, General Electric Company.
Bauer, Richard W., Associate Executive, Synod of Michigan, UPCUSA.
Beimler, George, Pastor, First Presbyterian Church, Liberty, New York.
Biersdorf, John, Director, Department of Ministry, National Council of the Churches of Christ in the U.S.A.
Brown, Thomas E., Director, Northeast Career Center, Princeton, New Jersey.
Carson, Charles Edgar, Acting Director, Executive and Field Service Commission, UPCUSA.
Clark, Donald, Chairman, Committee on Support of the Clergy, North Jersey Conference, United Church of Christ.
Cocks, Robert S., General Presbyter, Huntingdon and Northumberland Presbyteries, Pennsylvania Synod, UPCUSA.
De Beer, Leonard, Secretary for Professional Development, Reformed Church in America.
Deem, Warren, Consultant, Wilder Deem Associates, New York.
Dethmers, Vernon, Pastor, Community Church of Glen Rock, New Jersey.

220

Evans, Hugh Bean, Executive Secretary, Department of Ministerial Relations, UPCUSA.

Falkenberg, Don, Director-Counselor, Western Career Development Center, Oakland, California.

Forbes, Gordon, Pastor, First Congregational Church, Northfield, Minnesota.

Foulkes, Robert G., Secretary, Office of Church Occupations Counseling, Board of Christian Education, UPCUSA.

Gillespie, Thomas W., Pastor, First Presbyterian Church, Burlingame, California.

Hager, William Martin, Pastor, First Presbyterian Church, Pampa, Texas.

Harriman, Robert B., Executive Secretary, Department of Chaplains and Service Personnel, UPCUSA.

Harris, Jack, Director, Clergy Development Office, Diocese of Washington, D.C., The Episcopal Church.

Haversat, Albert L., Associate Secretary, Board of Theological Education, Lutheran Church in America.

Hawley, Ralph J., Associate Executive, Synod of Minnesota, UPCUSA.

Henderson, William H., Secretary for Vocation, Board of Christian Education, UPCUSA.

Herrold, Kenneth, Professor of Psychology, Teachers College, Columbia University.

Hoffman, Shad, Associate Dean, New York School of Social Work, Columbia University.

Illingworth, J. Davis, Executive, Golden Gate Synod, UPCUSA.

Irvine, Helen E., Personnel Manager, General Council, Board of National Missions, Commission on Ecumenical Mission and Relations, UPCUSA.

Jackson, Mance, Director of Field Work, Interdenominational Theological Center, Atlanta, Georgia.

Kerr, Robert, Associate Executive Secretary, Department of Ministerial Relations, UPCUSA.

Little, G. Daniel, Coordinator of Planning, Board of National Missions, UPCUSA.

Little, James S., Senior Pastor, Lafayette-Orinda United Presbyterian Church, Lafayette, California.

MacFarlane, Robert S., Jr., Associate Chairman, Division of Evangelism, Board of National Missions, UPCUSA.

Maier, Frederick C., Executive Coordinator, Department of Strategic Studies, Board of National Missions, UPCUSA.

Martin, James Payson, Pastor, Tabernacle Presbyterian Church, Indianapolis, Indiana.

Matthew, Glenn E., Superintendent of Ministries, Kansas Area, The United Methodist Church.

Matthew, John C., Chairman, Division of Leadership Development, Board of National Missions, UPCUSA.

Mead, Loren, Director, Project Test Pattern, The Episcopal Church.

Meister, John, Executive Secretary, Council of Theological Seminaries, UPCUSA.

Mills, Edgar W., Director, Ministry Studies Board, Washington, D.C.

Moore, Richard E., Associate Executive, Synod of Ohio, UPCUSA.

Muir, James W., Executive Presbyter, West Jersey Presbytery, UPCUSA.

Newbold, Robert T., Jr., Associate Executive Secretary, Department of Ministerial Relations, UPCUSA.

Rasmussen, Robert D., Director, Commission on the Ministry, American Baptist Convention, Valley Forge, Pennsylvania.

Reed, Robert H., Associate Executive, Synod of Oregon, UPCUSA.

Roberts, Alcwyn L., Associate Secretary, General Council, UPCUSA.

Rouch, Mark A., Associate Director, Department of the Ministry, Division of Higher Education, United Methodist Board of Education.

Samler, Joseph, United States Veterans Administration.

Skadra, Gordon H., Administrative Secretary for Mission Development Cabinet; Associate for Local Church Strategy, Board of National Missions, UPCUSA.

Skirvin, Sidney D., Dean of Students and Director of Placement, Union Theological Seminary, New York.

Smith, Carl R., Executive Presbyter, Genesee Valley Presbytery, Synod of New York, UPCUSA.

Sobel, Paul, Presbytery Executive, Presbytery of Monmouth, Synod of New Jersey, UPCUSA.

Story, Walter, Management Development Institute, General Electric Company.

Super, Donald E., Professor of Psychology, Teachers College, Columbia University.

Sweet, Herman J., Retired Field Director, Board of Christian Education, UPCUSA.

Timmons, Eugene E., Director, Career Support Services (Kansas and Missouri), UPCUSA.

Trubee, Franklin L., Minister of Mission, Presbytery of Wooster, Synod of Ohio, UPCUSA.

Walrath, Douglas A., Field Secretary, Synod of Albany, Reformed Church in America.

Wells, Robert L., Vice-President, Management and Professional Personnel, Westinghouse Electric Corporation.

White, Ronald T., Secretary, Board of Pensions, UPCUSA.

Williams, Frank C., Director, Midwest Career Development Center, Columbus, Ohio.

Womack, James T., Jr., Board of National Ministries, Presbyterian Church in the United States.

Worley, Robert C., Professor, McCormick Theological Seminary, Chicago, Illinois.

Wright, Paul S., Pastor, First Presbyterian Church, Portland, Oregon.

BIBLIOGRAPHY

* Titles so marked were read in abstract form and not in the original.

1. Academy of Parish Clergy, Inc., *Characteristics of the Professional.* No date. 7 pp.
2. ——— *Competence in the Parish Ministry.* 1971. Mimeographed. 2 pp.
3. ——— *Guidelines for Colleague Groups.* 1971. 7 pp.
4. ——— *Guidelines for Supervisor-Evaluators.* No date. 2 pp.
5. ——— *Learning from Each Other (Explorations of Clergy-Collegiality).* 1971. 7 pp.
6. Adams, Henry B., *The Collegial Model of Ministry.* Academy of of Parish Clergy, Inc. No date. 8 pp.
7. Adams, Henry Babcock, "Performance Evaluation in Ministry," *Theological Education,* Winter, 1971, pp. 102–108.
8. ——— "Consultation: An Alternative to Supervision," *Developments,* Department of Ministry, National Council of the Churches of Christ, Vol. III, No. 2 (June, 1968), pp. 1–5.
9. Anderson, James D., "Pastoral Support of Clergy-Role Development Within Local Congregations," *Pastoral Psychology,* Vol. XXII, No. 212 (March, 1971), pp. 9–14.
10. Argyris, Chris, *Integrating the Individual and the Organization.* John Wiley & Sons, Inc., 1964. 330 pp.
11. Ashbrook, James B., "Discussion of Hadden Paper," *Ministry Studies,* Vol. II, Nos. 3, 4 (Oct. and Dec., 1968), pp. 30–36.
12. ——— "Ministerial Leadership in Church Organization," *Ministry Studies,* Vol. I, No. 1 (May, 1967), pp. 5–32.
13. Bennett, Thomas R., "Can the Minister Risk Role Change?" *Ministry Studies,* Vol. II, No. 1 (Feb., 1968), pp. 27–29.

14. ——— "Discussion of Sam Blizzard's Paper," in Samuel Southard (ed.), *Conference on Motivation for the Ministry,* pp. 72–82. Louisville, Ky., Southern Baptist Seminary, 1959.

15. Bertalanffy, Ludwig von, *General System Theory: Foundations, Development, Applications.* George Braziller, Inc., 1969. 289 pp.

16. Blizzard, Samuel W., "The Minister's Dilemma," *The Christian Century,* Vol. LXXIII (1956), pp. 508–509.

17. ——— "The Parish Minister's Self-image of His Master Role," *Pastoral Psychology,* Vol. IX, No. 89 (Dec., 1958), pp. 25–32.

18. ——— "The Protestant Parish Minister's Integrating Roles," *Religious Education,* Vol. 53, No. 4 (July–Aug., 1958), pp. 374–380.

19. ——— "Role Conflicts of the Urban Ministry," *The City Church,* Vol. VII (1956), No. 4, pp. 13–15.

20. Board of National Missions, The United Presbyterian Church U.S.A., *A Guide for the Development of Standards for Personnel Policies and Practices.* A mimeographed working draft. 1970. 94 pp.

21. ——— *Mission Review Guide.* 1969. 24 pp.

22. Bowers, Margaretta K., M.D., *Conflicts of the Clergy: A Psychodynamic Study with Case Histories.* Thomas Nelson & Sons, 1963. 252 pp.

23. Broadus, Loren, "A Constructive Approach to Frustration in the Practice of Ministry," *Pastoral Psychology,* Vol. XXII, No. 213 (April, 1971), pp. 39–44.

24. Brown, Thomas, "Career Counseling as a Form of Pastoral Care," *Pastoral Psychology,* Vol. XXII, No. 212 (March, 1971), pp. 15–20.

25. ——— "Career Counseling for Ministers," *Journal of Pastoral Care,* Vol. XXV, No. 1 (March, 1971), pp. 33–40.

26. ——— "Vocational Crises and Occupational Satisfaction Among Ministers," *Princeton Seminary Bulletin,* Vol. LXIII, Nos. 2–3 (December, 1970), pp. 52–62.

27. Carson, Charles E., *Guidelines for the Review and Preview of Work and Work Objectives.* Executive and Field Service Commission, The United Presbyterian Church U.S.A., Jan., 1971. Mimeographed. 5 pp.

*28. Chamberlain, D. B., "Communication Problems in the Parish Ministry: An Action Research Study of Fifty Protestant Ministers in a New England City," Ph.D., Boston University, 1958. *Dissertation Abstracts,* 19:891–892 (1958).

29. Christman, Earl S., *Evaluation Questions for Use by Session.* Nov. 25, 1967.

30. Coates, Charles H., and Kistler, Robert C., "Role Dilemmas of

Protestant Clergymen in a Metropolitan Community," *Review of Religious Research,* Vol. VI, No. 3 (Spring, 1965), pp. 147–152.

*31. Colwell, C. A., "Roles and Role Conflicts of the Parish Minister." Ph.D., The Hartford Seminary Foundation, 1964. *Dissertation Abstracts,* 25:4271 (Jan., 1965).

32. Coop, Robert, and others, *Strengthening Employee Performance Evaluation.* Personnel Report No. 663. Chicago, Public Personnel Association. No date. 46 pp.

33. DeBoer, John C., *Let's Plan: A Guide to the Planning Process for Voluntary Organizations.* Pilgrim Press, 1970. 182 pp.

34. Department of Ministerial Relations, The United Presbyterian Church U.S.A., *Manual for Ministerial Relationships in the Local Church.* No date. Mimeographed. 19 pp.

*35. Didier, James William, "The Role of the Baptist Parish Minister in the State of Michigan," Ph.D., Michigan State University, 1965. *Dissertation Abstracts,* 26:4840 (Feb., 1966).

36. Dittes, James E., *Minister on the Spot.* Pilgrim Press, 1970. 138 pp.

37. —— "To Accept and To Celebrate Conflict," *Ministry Studies,* Vol. II, Nos. 3, 4 (Oct. and Dec., 1968), pp. 43–46.

38. Division of Church Strategy and Development, Board of National Missions, The United Presbyterian Church U.S.A., *Guide to the Exploration of Mission in the Local Congregation.* No date. Loose-leaf. 103 pp.

39. Division of Evangelism, Board of National Missions, The United Presbyterian Church U.S.A., and the Division of Evangelism, Board for Homeland Ministries, United Church of Christ, *Guidelines for the Development of Local Church Clusters.* May, 1970. 21 pp.

40. Donovan, J. J., *Problems and Pitfalls in Employee Performance Evaluation.* Personnel Brief Series, No. 27. Chicago, Public Personnel Association, 1964. 16 pp.

41. Drucker, Peter F., *The Practice of Management.* Harper & Row, Publishers, Inc., 1954. 404 pp.

42. Eggleston, Donald, and Snyder, Robert T., "The Priest's Role as Seen by Seminarians and Faculty," *Catholic Educational Review,* Vol. LXVI (1969), No. 10, pp. 617–631.

43. Episcopal Church, The, Strategic Research Services Group of the Executive Council, *The Top Priority Empirical Research Project on the Clergy.* Darien, Conn., Ecumenical Consultants, Inc., 1970. Contains 11 reports. 226 pp.

*44. Falk, L. L., "The Minister's Response to His Perception of Conflict

Between Self-Expectations and Parishioners' Expectations of His Role," Ph.D., The University of Nebraska, 1962. *Dissertation Abstracts,* 23:2611–2612 (Jan., 1963).

45. Fichter, Joseph H., *Religion as an Occupation.* University of Notre Dame Press, 1966. 295 pp.

46. Fletcher, John, and Edwards, Tilden, Jr., "A Metropolitan Approach to Interfaith Theological Education." Washington, D.C., Inter-Met. No date. Mimeographed. 15 pp.

47. Forbes, Gordon, *Building a Shared Ministry in a Local Church.* 1972. Typed manuscript. 9 pp.

48. French, William H., *Planning, Budgeting, Evaluating System for Judicatories and Agencies.* The United Presbyterian Church U.S.A., 1972. 38 pp.

49. Friedmann, Eugene A., and Havighurst, Robert J., *The Meaning of Work and Retirement.* The University of Chicago Press, 1954. 197 pp.

50. Fukuyama, Yoshio, "Changes in Role Expectations: A Sociologist's Commentary," *Ministry Studies,* Vol. II, No. 1 (Feb., 1968), pp. 24–26.

51. —— *The Parishioners: A Sociological Interpretation.* Research Department, Board for Homeland Ministries, United Church of Christ, 1966. Mimeographed. 42 pp.

52. —— *Preachers and Seminarians: A Profession in Transition.* No date. Mimeographed. 20 pp.

53. Gannon, Thomas M., S.J., "Priest/Minister: Profession or Non-Profession?" *Review of Religious Research,* Vol. XII, No. 2 (Winter, 1971), pp. 66–79.

54. Gilbert, Wyn, *Standards for Executive Performance for Associate Synod Executives, Synod of Washington-Alaska.* Synod of Washington-Alaska, June 1, 1970. Mimeographed.

55. Glasse, James D., "Implications for Ministry—Interpretive Comments," *Ministry Studies,* Vol. I, No. 1 (May, 1967), pp. 33–36.

56. —— *Profession: Minister.* Abingdon Press, 1968. 174 pp.

*57. Glock, C. Y., and Ringer, B. B., "Parish Policy and the Attitudes of Ministers and Parishioners on Social Issues," *American Sociological Review,* Vol. XXI (1956), pp. 148–156. Abstract of this article appears in Menges, Robert J., and Dittes, James E., *Psychological Studies of Clergymen: Abstracts of Research.* Thomas Nelson & Sons, 1965, p. 77.

58. Gravengaard, Karen L. (ed.), *Findings,* Nov.–Dec., 1969, "PAOM

. . . Ministry and Management." Office of Study and Research, Board of Christian Education, The United Presbyterian Church U.S.A.

59. Gross, Neal; Mason, Ward S.; and McEachern, A. W., *Explorations in Role Analysis: Studies of the School Superintendency Role.* John Wiley & Sons, Inc., 1958. 379 pp.

60. Gustafson, James M., "An Analysis of the Problem of the Role of the Minister," *Journal of Religion,* Vol. XXXIV (1954), No. 3, pp. 187–191.

61. Hadden, Jeffrey K., *The Gathering Storm in the Churches: A Sociologist's View of the Widening Gap Between Clergy and Laymen.* Doubleday & Company, Inc., 1969. 257 pp.

62. ———— "Role Conflict and the Crisis in the Churches," *Ministry Studies,* Vol. II, Nos. 3, 4 (Oct. and Dec., 1968), pp. 16–29.

63. ———— "A Study of the Protestant Ministry of America," *Journal for the Scientific Study of Religion,* Vol. V, No. 1 (Oct., 1965), pp. 10–23.

64. Hager, Martin, *Performance Appraisal Systems for the Parish Ministry.* Plains Presbytery (UPCUSA), April, 1969. Mimeographed. 28 pp.

65. Harris, John C., "New Trends in Pastoral Care for Pastors," *Pastoral Psychology,* Vol. XXII, No. 212 (March, 1971), pp. 5–8.

66. Hartford Seminary Foundation, The, *A Proposal for Support of Christian Ministry.* Dec., 1971.

67. Haversat, Albert L., *Career Evaluation and Planning for Ministers.* Issue paper for the Annual Conference of Synodical Presidents, Detroit, Mich., Feb. 16–18, 1971.

68. Hawley, Ralph J., *Rationale for Local Church Personnel Committees.* Address on March 10–11, 1972. Mimeographed. 7 pp.

69. Henderson, William, *Candidates and Career Counseling: A Report.* 1970. Mimeographed. 3 pp.

70. Hesser, Gary W., and Mills, Edgar W., *An Empirical Study of Protestant Clergymen: With Special Attention to Their Involvement in Continuing Education.* A paper presented at the annual meeting of the Society for the Advancement of Continuing Education for Ministers, June, 1971. Mimeographed. 18 pp.

71. Higgins, Paul S., and Dittes, James E., "Change in Laymen's Expectations of the Minister's Role," *Ministry Studies,* Vol. II, No. 1 (Feb., 1968), pp. 5–8.

72. Howe, Reuel L., "Theological Education and the Image of the Min-

istry," in Keith R. Bridston and Dwight W. Culver (eds.), *The Making of Ministers: Essays on Clergy Training Today,* pp. 207–227. Augsburg Publishing House, 1964.

73. Interdenominational Theological Center, *Continuing Education Program for Black Clergy.* Atlanta, Ga. No date. Typewritten document. 22 pp.

74. Jud, Gerald L., and others, *Ex-Pastors: Why Men Leave the Parish Ministry.* Pilgrim Press, 1970. 191 pp.

75. Jurgensen, Clifford E., and others, *Employee Performance Appraisal Re-examined.* Personnel Report No. 613. Chicago, Public Personnel Association. No date. 29 pp.

76. Kahn, Robert L., and others, *Organizational Stress: Studies in Role Conflict and Ambiguity.* John Wiley & Sons, Inc., 1964. 470 pp.

77. Katz, Daniel, and Kahn, Robert L., *The Social Psychology of Organizations.* John Wiley & Sons, Inc., 1966. 498 pp.

78. Kelly, Sheila M., and others, *Who Do Men Say that I Am? A Report on Identity and the Parish Priest in The Episcopal Church.* Strategic Research Services Group, Executive Council of The Episcopal Church, 1970. 13 pp.

79. Kennedy, Eugene C., "Psychological Consequences in Role Conflict Among Clergy," *Ministry Studies,* Vol. II, Nos. 3, 4 (Oct. and Dec., 1968), pp. 50–51.

80. Kennedy, Gerald, *The Seven Worlds of the Minister.* Harper & Row, Publishers, Inc., 1968. 173 pp.

81. Kennedy, James W., *Minister's Shop-Talk.* Harper & Row, Publishers, Inc., 1965. 211 pp.

82. Kinnane, John F., *Career Development for Priests and Religious.* Washington, D.C., Center for Applied Research in the Apostolate, 1970. 133 pp.

83. Kling, Frederick R., *Roles of the Parish Minister.* Princeton, Educational Testing Service, 1959. Mimeographed document. 5 pp.

84. ———— "A Study of Testing as Related to the Ministry," *Religious Education,* Vol. LIII, May–June, 1958, pp. 243–248.

*85. Kolarik, J. M., "A Study of the Critical Requirements of the Lutheran Ministry." Ph.D., University of Pittsburgh, 1954. *Dissertation Abstracts,* 14:2395–2396 (1954).

86. Lafayette-Orinda United Presbyterian Church, Lafayette, California. *Report to the Session of the Results of the Congregational Questionnaire.* June, 1970. Mimeographed. 35 pp.

87. Lee, Ronald R., "The Practice of Ministry," *Journal of Pastoral Care,* Vol. XXVI, No. 1 (March, 1972), pp. 33–39.

88. Leiffer, Murray H., *Changing Expectations and Ethics in the Professional Ministry.* Bureau of Social and Religious Research, Garrett Theological Seminary, 1969. 189 pp.

89. Levinson, Harry, "Management by Whose Objectives?" *Harvard Business Review,* July–Aug., 1970, pp. 125–134.

90. Lopez, Felix M., *Evaluating Employee Performance.* Chicago, Public Personnel Association, 1968. 299 pp.

91. Lutheran Church in America, Personnel Support Service, *Instruction Manual.* No date. 34 pp.

92. Mahler, Walter R., "A Systems Approach to Managing by Objectives," *Systems and Procedures Journal.* Vol. XVI, No. 5 (Sept.–Oct., 1965).

93. Maier, Frederick C., "The 'Nature of the Ministry' Seminars: A Report and Evaluation," *McCormick Quarterly,* Vol. XVII (1963), No. 3, pp. 20–29.

94. Mead, Loren B., *New Hope for Congregations.* The Seabury Press, Inc., forthcoming.

95. —— *The Parish Is the Issue: A Report and a Proposal.* Project Test Pattern, National Advisory Committee on Evangelism, The Episcopal Church, 1970. Mimeographed. 19 pp.

96. —— *The Vacancy Consultation Project.* Project Test Pattern, 1972. Mimeographed. 6 pp.

97. Menges, Robert J., and Dittes, James E., *Psychological Studies of Clergymen: Abstracts of Research.* Thomas Nelson & Sons, 1965. 202 pp.

98. Menges, Robert J., "Studies of Clergymen: Abstracts of Research, Supplement 1," *Ministry Studies,* Vol. I, No. 3 (Oct., 1967). 79 pp.

99. Merton, Robert K., *Social Theory and Social Structure,* enl. ed. The Free Press, 1968. 702 pp.

100. Meyer, Herbert H., and others, "Split Roles in Performance Appraisal," *Harvard Business Review,* Jan.–Feb., 1965, pp. 123–129.

101. Mills, Edgar W., *Career Change Among Ministers.* Harvard Studies in Career Development, No. 46. Center for Research in Careers, Graduate School of Education, Harvard University, 1966. 177 pp.

102. —— "A Career Development in Middle Life," in Willis E. Bartlett (ed.), *Evolving Religious Careers,* pp. 181–198. Washington, D.C., Center for Applied Research in the Apostolate, 1970.

103. —— "The Assessment of Readiness for Ministry." May 10, 1971. Draft document, Xeroxed. 9 pp.

104. —— *Relating Objectives and Evaluation.* Henry B. Adams (ed.), Proceedings of the Adult Learning Seminar, Department of Min-

istry, National Council of the Churches of Christ in the U.S.A., 1967. Mimeographed.

105. —— "Types of Role Conflict Among Clergymen," *Ministry Studies,* Vol. II, Nos. 3, 4 (Oct. and Dec., 1968), pp. 13–15.

106. Mills, Edgar W., and Koval, John P., *Stress in the Ministry.* New York, Ministry Studies Board and IDOC, 1971. 70 pp.

107. Morton, Robert B., "Leveling with Others on the Job." American Management Association. Reprinted from *Personnel Magazine,* Nov.–Dec., 1966. 6 pp.

108. Office of Human Resources, Reformed Church in America, *A Personnel Development Interview Program for the Minister.* 1972. 22 pp.

109. Office of Planning and Research of the General Council, The United Presbyterian Church U.S.A., *Planning in the Church,* 1971. 17 pp.

*110. Plyler, Henry E., "Variation of Ministerial Roles by Size and Location of Church." Ph.D., University of Missouri, 1961. *Dissertation Abstracts,* 22:2904–2905 (Feb., 1962).

111. Presbyterian Church in Willingboro, N.J., *Performance Appraisal Plan.* 5 pp.

112. Presbyteries of Northwest Missouri and Topeka-Highlands (UPCUSA), *Manual for Salary Review and Performance Appraisal.* 1970.

113. Presbytery of Genesee Valley (UPCUSA), Documents for Churches Seeking Financial Support. Jan. 6, 1970.

114. —— *Executive Performance Review and Preview.* Oct. 7, 1970. Xeroxed document. 4 pp.

115. —— *Goal-Setting and Evaluation for Pastor and Session.* June, 1969. Mimeographed. 3 pp.

116. Presbytery of Hudson River (UPCUSA), *Performance Review.* 1969. Mimeographed. 1 p.

117. Presbytery of Indianapolis (UPCUSA), *Guidelines for Using the Pastoral Performance Record.* No date. 1 p.

118. —— *Pastoral Performance Record.* No date. 1 p.

119. Project Test Pattern, *Design AA-20, The Parish Intervention Handbook.* Washington, D.C., P.T.P., 1971.

120. Public Personnel Association, "A Rating System to Improve Job Performance," *Personnel Report No. 651.* No date. 12 pp.

121. Pusey, Nathan M., and others, *Ministry for Tomorrow: Report of the Special Committee on Theological Education.* Protestant Episcopal Church in the U.S.A. The Seabury Press, Inc., 1967. 142 pp.

122. Rouch, Mark A., "Young Pastors Pilot Project: An Experiment in

Continuing Education for Ministry," *Journal of Pastoral Care,* Vol. XXV, No. 1 (March, 1971), pp. 3–11.

123. Sarbin, Theodore R., and Allen, Vernon L., "Role Theory," in Lindzey, Gardner, and Aronson, Elliot (eds.), *The Handbook of Social Psychology,* 2d ed. Addison-Wesley Publishing Company, Inc., 1968, Vol. I, pp. 488–567.

124. Scherer, Ross P., "The Lutheran Ministry: Origins, Careers, Self-appraisals," *Information Service,* Vol. XLII, April 27, 1963, pp. 1–8.

125. Schneider, Benjamin, and Hall, Douglas T., "The Role of Assignment Characteristics in the Career Experiences of Diocesan Priests," in Willis E. Bartlett (ed.), *Evolving Religious Careers.* Washington, D.C., Center for Applied Research in the Apostolate, 1970, pp. 101–132.

126. Smart, James D., *The Rebirth of Ministry.* The Westminster Press, 1960. 192 pp.

127. Smith, Donald P., *Counselor's Handbook, Personnel Development Program.* Commission on Ecumenical Mission and Relations, The United Presbyterian Church U.S.A., 1969. 117 pp.

128. ——— "Personnel Development Interviews: A Step in the Direction of Personnel Policies for the 21st Century?" *Occasional Bulletin,* Vol. XXI, No. 9 (Sept. 1970), pp. 1–23.

129. Smith, Luke Mader, "Paris Clergymen's Role Images as Pastoral Counselors," *Journal of Pastoral Care,* Vol. XIV, No. 1 (Spring, 1960), pp. 21–28.

130. Stewart, Charles W., "What Frustrates a Minister," *Christian Advocate,* Vol. IX (1965), No. 1, pp. 9–10.

131. Super, Donald E., *The Psychology of Careers.* Harper & Brothers, 1957. 362 pp.

132. ——— and others, *Career Development: Self-concept Theory.* College Entrance Examination Board, 1963. 95 pp.

133. ——— and others, *Vocational Development: A Framework for Research.* Teachers College, Columbia University, 1957. 142 pp.

134. Synod of Albany, Reformed Church in America, *A Progress Report on Church Renewal in the Synod of Albany.* 1971. Mimeographed. 32 pp.

135. Synod of Michigan (UPCUSA), *Staff Objectives and Performance Program (STOPP).* 1970. 11 pp.

136. Synod of Ohio (UPCUSA), *Guide to Planned Accomplishments in the Synod of Ohio.* No date. Offset form. 4 pp.

137. Synod of Oregon (UPCUSA), *Digest of the Care and Oversight Conference.* Willamette Presbytery, Sept. 11–12, 1970. 4 pp.

138. Thompson, James D., and Van Houten, Donald R., *The Behavioral Sciences: An Interpretation.* Addison-Wesley Publishing Company, Inc., 1970. 268 pp.

139. Thompson, Paul H., and Dalton, Gene W., "Performance Appraisal: Managers Beware." *Harvard Business Review,* Vol. XLVIII, No. 1 (Jan.–Feb., 1970), pp. 149–157.

140. Timmons, Eugene E., *Judicatory Pastoral Career Support.* No date. 10 pp.

141. Trubee, Franklin L., and Dreyer, E. C., *Guide to Planned Professional Accomplishments.* No date. Mimeographed form. 5 pp.

142. Veterans Administration, *Quality Requirements for the Several Types of Counseling End Products.* M7-1. Mar. 30, 1959. p. II 60–68.

143. Washington Episcopal Clergy Association, *Professional Responsibilities and Standards.* Adopted Nov. 9, 1970.

144. Whisler, Thomas L., and Harper, Shirley F. (eds.), *Performance Appraisal, Research and Practice.* Holt, Rinehart & Winston, Inc., 1962. 593 pp.

145. Whitlock, Glen E., "Role and Self-concepts in the Choice of the Ministry as a Vocation," *Journal of Pastoral Care,* Vol. XVII, No. 4 (Winter, 1963), pp. 208–212.

146. Williams, Frank C., *Some Perspectives on the Needs of Clergy— Personal and Professional.* Midwest Career Development Center, Sept., 1970. Mimeographed. 22 pp.

147. Wilson, Robert L., "Drop-Outs and Potential Drop-Outs from Parish Ministry," *Review of Religious Research,* Vol. XII, No. 3 (Spring, 1971), p. 188.

*148. Wood, C. L., "Functions of the Parish Priest in the Episcopal Diocese of New Jersey," Ed.D., Rutgers—The State University, 1964. *Dissertation Abstracts,* 25:2870 (Nov., 1964).

149. Woodward, Albert T., and others, *Performance Review of Clergy, Prepared for the Presbytery of Monmouth* [UPCUSA]. June, 1969. 12 pp.